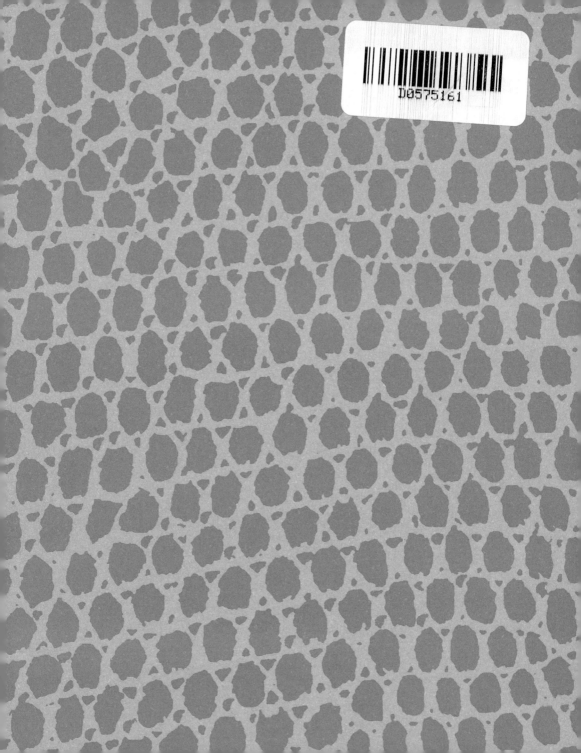

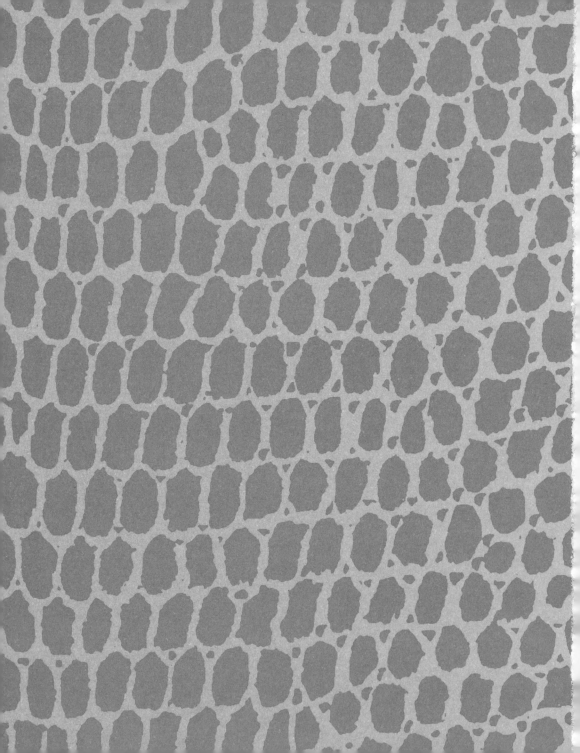

Freshwater
Aquarium
Problem
Solver

DAVID E. BORUCHOWITZ

Freshwater Aquarium Problem Solver

Project Team
Editor: Brian Scott
Copy Editor:Mary Connell
Series Design: Stephanie Krautheim & Leah Lococo Ltd.
Design: Mary Ann Kahn

T.F.H. Publications
President/CEO: Glen S.Axelrod
Executive Vice President: Mark E. Johnson
Publisher: Christopher T. Reggio
Production Manager: Kathy Bontz

T.F.H. Publications, Inc.
One TFH PlazaThird and Union Avenues
Neptune City, NJ 07753

Discovery Communications, Inc. Book Development Team:
Maureen Smith, Executive Vice President & General
    Manager, Animal Planet
Carol LeBlanc,Vice President, Marketing and Retail
    Development
Elizabeth Bakacs,Vice President, Creative Services
Peggy Ang, Director, Animal Planet Marketing
Caitlin Erb, Marketing Associate

Printed and bound in China
06 07 08 09 10 1 3 5 7 9 8 6 4 2

Library of Congress Cataloging-in-Publication Data
Freshwater aquarium problem solver / David E. Boruchowitz.
p. cm.
Includes bibliographical references and index.
ISBN 0-7938-3761-8 (alk. paper)
1. Aquariums. 2. Aquarium fishes. 3. Aquarium plants. I.Title.
SF457.3.B68 2006
639.34–dc22
2006013104

This book has been published with the intent to provide accurate and authoritative information in regard to the subject matter
within.While every precaution has been taken in preparation of this book, the author and publisher expressly disclaim responsibility for any errors, omissions, or adverse effects arising from the use or application of the information contained herein.The tech-
niques and suggestions are used at the reader's discretion and are not to be considered a substitute for veterinary care. If you sus-
pect a medical problem consult your veterinarian.

The Leader In Responsible Animal Care For Over 50 Years!™
www.tfhpublications.com

Table of **Contents**

Introduction

Most introductory books on aquariums concentrate on telling you how to do things so that your setup works properly and you can enjoy your fish. Unfortunately, things can go wrong, even if you follow instructions, and especially if you don't. Either way, you can wind up with a problem that wasn't described in a book.

Well, that's where this book comes in. The common problems a new fishkeeper might face have been gathered and described, along with the way to fix the problems. The book is organized into chapters according to the types of problems a hobbyist may face, and each chapter goes into detail about how to prevent them as well as deal with them if they occur.

Chapter 1

Tank Cycling Problems Solved!

Almost all the problems that new aquarists have with cycling stem from misunderstanding. No other aspect of the aquarium hobby is as surrounded in unnecessary mystery as is tank cycling. People treat it like a secret ritual, whose rites must be followed exactly to the letter. While cycling is somewhat mystifying, it is very important and actually fairly straightforward.

The cause of all the misunderstanding undoubtedly stems from the fact that the many processes involved are all invisible. Except for taking readings from your test kit, you cannot see what is happening nor determine if things are proceeding normally. Since you have no direct way of knowing if the advice you receive is good or not, you must take it on faith.

What Is Cycling Anyway?

Cycling a tank refers to establishing a functioning biofilter. A biofilter is a special bacterial colony growing in some medium through which the aquarium water is directed to pass. These bacteria are of two types. The first consume ammonia, turning it into nitrite. Ammonia is extremely toxic to fish, and nitrite is quite toxic. The second type of bacteria convert nitrite into nitrate. Nitrate is toxic only in large concentrations. Thus, a biofilter takes a very poisonous waste and turns it into a much less harmful substance in a two-step process. The accumulated nitrate is then diluted whenever a water change is performed.

The process is called "cycling" because it sets up part of the nitrogen cycle in the aquarium. The details of the whole complex topic aren't important, since in an aquarium, only a small portion is significant, namely the breakdown of ammonia and nitrite by certain bacteria. These bacteria are necessary for the biofilter, and they themselves have three basic needs: surface area, nutrients, and oxygen.

Surface Area

Biofiltration bacteria do not live free in the water; they must attach to a substrate. They will grow on just about any surface—the glass, plant leaves, gravel grains. To encourage the large colonies that are needed, biofilters contain a medium that has a high concentration of microscopic surface area. High-quality activated carbon is probably the medium that contains the largest micropore surface area, but

Lava chips provide a perfect substrate for beneficial bacteria to colonize.

there are many other excellent media, including ceramic foam, foam sponge, and even the regular polyester fiber used for mechanical filtration. Anything that provides microscopic surface area and is in the flow of aquarium water will be colonized by the bacteria. This includes anything used for mechanical filtration, although the surface area in mechanical filters is typically not sufficient to handle the tank's bioload.

Nutrients

One type of biofiltration bacteria eats ammonia, and the other type eats nitrite. If these substances are available in the water, the bacteria will form colonies and establish a working biofilter. In fact, it is by tracking the concentrations of these nutrients that the cycling process can be monitored.

Oxygen

Since these beneficial bacteria require oxygen, the biomedium must be provided with an uninterrupted supply of oxygen. There are some easy ways of doing this.

Oxygen can be provided simply by keeping a large volume of the aquarium water flowing over the biomedium.

Alternately, many biofilters take advantage of the fact that atmospheric air contains about 20,000 times the oxygen of the best oxygenated water. Therefore, a very thin film of water, only a few molecules thick, will,

Hang-on style power filters often have bio-wheels, which help to aerate and cleanse the water.

in the presence of air, maintain a much higher steady oxygen concentration—in effect, it's a water surface without a body of water below it. As the bacteria use up the oxygen in the water, it is immediately replaced. This is accomplished by not submerging the biomedium in water; instead the water sprays, dribbles, or trickles over or through the medium, collecting below the medium for return to the aquarium. Because this type of filter has a body of water and a compartment that does not hold water but is merely kept wet, it is referred to—with just a touch of poetic license—as a "wet-dry filter." The amount of medium needed to maintain an adequate bacterial colony is much less for a wet-dry system then for a flow-through one.

Several hang-on power filters include having the water drip onto rotating biowheels or through a sponge medium above the water line as the last stage. These effectively combine a wet-dry biofilter into the system.

How Does It Work?

In reality, it's not a tank that is cycled, it's a biofilter that is matured. We can therefore phrase the question of how cycling works as: "How does a biofilter mature?"

The best answer to keep in mind is: Slowly, over time. Patience is extremely important. Cycling can take as long as six weeks or more. It is a terrible temptation to have an aquarium all set up and running with only a couple of fish in it; the urge is to fully stock it, but you must resist the desire to get more fish.

The only tools needed are your ammonia, nitrite, and nitrate test kits. Read their instructions carefully and make sure you know how to use them. Somewhere there will be a chart, probably with three levels designated as: safe, concern, and danger. In the cycling process, many readings have to be in the midrange—more than negligible but not yet toxic. This is because in order for the bacteria to grow, they have to have food (ammonia and nitrite). If the levels were to get into the danger zone, cycling would continue, at a faster rate, but the fish in the tank would die.

Good Bugs

Bacteria are the predominant life form on Earth, whether measured by numbers, weight, or any other metric. Many species of bacteria are not just beneficial, but necessary—like the bacteria living in your intestines, without which you would die. Biofiltration bacteria are likewise required in a healthy aquarium.

The fish you choose to begin cycling your tank should be hardy types that can withstand the moderate levels of ammonia and nitrite that will occur. Zebra danios are excellent, as are guppies or platies. More sensitive species can be added later, when your aquarium conditions are as described in Stage Three below.

THE CYCLING PROCESS

Every tank is different, so we cannot give anything other than general guidelines, but the proper protocol for cycling a tank/maturing a biofilter contains three stages:

Stage One

Once the aquarium is set up, introduce two or three hardy fish. Do not feed them at all for a day or two. This limits how much ammonia they will produce.

Test the water for ammonia. If it is not at the dangerous level, feed the fish a small amount.

The next day, test the water for ammonia. If it is not at the dangerous level, feed the fish a small amount. If it is in the danger zone, do not feed the fish, and perform a water change to bring the ammonia level back into the safe range.

After a week or so, check for nitrite. If there is none, wait a few days and test again. Once there is measurable nitrite, you have moved on to Stage Two.

Stage Two

Test the water for ammonia and nitrite. If they are not at the dangerous level, feed the fish a small amount. If either is in the danger zone, do not feed the fish, and perform a water change to bring the level back into the safe range. Repeat daily.

At some point the ammonia level will drop to zero. This indicates that the first type of bacteria have become established and are consuming all of the ammonia as it is produced. Nitrite will continue to rise until the second type of bacteria become established. Because a new biofilter is unstable, there may be an ammonia spike during this stage, so although it is not necessary to check ammonia every day when you check the nitrite level, you should occasionally also test the ammonia.

When the ammonia remains at zero and the nitrite begins to fall, nitrate will begin to accumulate. You can check that with your test kit. When both ammonia and nitrite remain at zero, you can move on to Stage Three.

Stage Three

At this point, many people make the mistake of thinking that cycling is done. This is true only in terms of the number of fish you have in the tank. That is, the biofilter is able to handle the wastes produced by those fish. When you add more fish, you will increase the bioload, and the filter may or may not be able to handle the increase without dangerous spikes in ammonia or nitrite.

Therefore, you should only gradually add more fish, a few at a time, until you have reached full stocking. Wait a week or so between additions, and test every other day or so. Never add more fish unless both ammonia and nitrite levels are at zero.

This gradual, three-stage protocol does require patience, but it ensures that you establish a fully mature biofilter without undue stress on your fish.

Isn't There an Easier Way?

Since this process is actually one of maturing a biofilter, not cycling a tank, this suggests that there must be an easier way to get a new tank started safely. There is: Borrow a biofilter! You can do this in several different ways.

11

Seeding a Biofilter

If you take some gravel or a few plants from an established aquarium and place them into your new tank, you will be "seeding" it with bacteria. This speeds up the maturation of your new biofilter, but it will still take time. If you have access to another aquarist's tank, this is a viable option.

Using Mature Media

It is possible to completely shortcut cycling if you borrow a complete biofilter. By using either all the media or the entire filter from an established tank, you can start with a mature biofilter. You cannot, of course, remove the entire biofiltration system from a tank; it will crash, needing to be cycled again. Many tanks have more than one biofilter, and eliminating one is usually not a problem. Of course, the old tank from which the biofilter is removed should be monitored for a while to make sure there are no ammonia or nitrite spikes, in which case water changes should be performed to keep the fish safe.

Using a Matured Filter

An aquarist friend or a friendly retailer can help you with a very simple plan. Take the new filter you are going to be using on your aquarium and set it up on one of their tanks as a supplemental filter. The best scenario or protocol would be to put your new filter in an overcrowded tank (which will benefit

from your filter's help) or one with a lot of heavy-feeding fish like large cichlids. Let the filter run on that tank for six weeks.

Then remove it and quickly—within a few minutes (so the bacterial colonies don't suffer from that lack of water flow)—install it on your tank. Plug it in, and you have a cycled tank! It is important to place several fish—about a half to two-thirds of the final stocking—into the tank right away. This will ensure enough nutrients to maintain the bacterial colonies. If after a couple of

Biofilters come in an assortment of shapes and sizes. This bio-tower is one example that is commonly employed in a large system.

Siphoning your gravel on a regular basis is crucial to maintaining a healthy balance in your aquarium.

days your ammonia and nitrite levels measure zero, you can add the rest of the fish. You should still check the levels every few days until you are certain that the biofilter is stable.

Common Questions about Cycling

People encounter many problems when cycling a tank, and there is an enormous amount of bad and misleading advice being passed around about how to solve these problems. Cycling *is* certainly confusing. Let's look at some common concerns.

What Is "New Tank Syndrome"?

New tank syndrome is an informal designation for a lack of understanding of biofiltration. It usually manifests as a newly-set-up aquarium, full of dead fish. When you fill a tank with water and then add fish, there is no biofilter, and within a couple days the fish all die from ammonia poisoning.

What about Water Changes?

Many people advise *against* water changes during cycling. They claim that they slow down the process by removing nutrients. Exactly! That's what water changes do—they remove harmful substances. True, during cycling you want to feed your growing biofilter, but you don't want to injure or kill your fish in the process!

Whenever ammonia or nitrite inch up into the toxic range, you need to perform a water change. Not a giant one, bringing the levels down to zero, but enough of a change to dilute the concentrations back into the safe range. This might indeed add a day or two to the cycling process, but, remember, patience is the key here.

Why Did My Ammonia Spike?

Often you will get a positive test for ammonia some time after it had stabilized at zero. An ammonia spike like this is often referred to as mini cycling. It may be caused by the instability of an immature biofilter,

SMALL FRY

Learning Patience

Children are naturally impatient. It is especially difficult for them to have an aquarium with only a couple of fish in it, waiting for this invisible process called "cycling" to take place. Involve them in the testing of the water, explaining what the test results have to be for it to be safe to add more fish. This will break the anticipation up into daily segments and help the time to pass before the tank can be fully stocked. And you may be surprised how much your child learns during the process.

which can vary from day to day in its ability to process wastes, but it can also be caused by an actual setback. If the tank got too warm or too cold, bacterial colonies may have died back, and they will require time to regrow. You may have added fish, or overfed a bit. Often the culprit is a dead fish wedged in where it cannot be easily seen.

The solution to this problem is the same as it is during cycling: do a water change to bring down the ammonia level, then test daily until things have again stabilized. When you do the water change, vacuum the gravel thoroughly and look around behind rocks and such for decomposing food, dead plants, or dead fish. As long as the existing fish in the tank look okay, they can stay in the tank. If they are showing signs of distress then they should be moved to a different, and more stable, setup.

Just because an aquarium is well-balanced now doesn't mean that it will remain so. Be sure to monitor your ammonia level on a weekly basis at least.

You should be on the lookout for an ammonia spike whenever you add fish to the tank, use medications, or have anything happen that might affect your biofilter. During the initial stocking, adding only a few fish at a time is the best way to make sure you never overtax the biofilter.

What Is the "Gradual Stocking Method" of Cycling?

In this method, one fish is added to the tank at a time, with a week or so between additions. Because so little bioload is added at any given time, the ammonia and nitrite levels rarely get into the danger zone. It takes longer to cycle, but it is much safer.

This is also a way to cycle a tank that is going to contain only species that normally could not survive cycling. The only other option is to use a different species, a tough one that will cycle the tank and that you can then replace with the desired species.

How Can Someone Get Away with Not Cycling Their Tank?

They can't. Let me point out that cycling is something that *happens*. It isn't something that you do.

Despite the shorthand phrasing that we use, *you* do not cycle the tank (mature the biofilter), the tank itself cycles (the biofilter itself matures).

Someone who sets up a tank and never picks up a test kit or worries about adding fish and somehow lucks out and doesn't lose any fish might mistakenly say, "I never cycled the tank." No, he didn't, but the tank cycled anyway. That is, a biofilter developed, and due to dumb luck, it developed quickly enough to save the fish from death (though perhaps not from injury or suffering).

But Is There Any Way to Completely Avoid Cycling?

There will always be a bit of biofiltration bacteria in a tank—on the glass if nothing else—but there is one way to have a successful tank without a biofilter beyond that. That is to have a flow-through system, like many commercial hatcheries. In such a setup, each tank is fitted with an overflow. When water reaches a certain level, it overflows and goes down the drain. Above each tank is a valve which introduces fresh water into the aquarium 24 hours a day.

This type of system can be quite expensive to run, since you must have a constant, massive supply of water at the right temperature. Of course, if you have a geothermal well, as one commercial cichlid breeder I know does, you can eliminate all filtration and heating and produce extremely healthy fish in perfectly clean water with the only expense being running the water pumps.

The flow rate must be high for this to work, since all ammonia has to be diluted and swept out of the tank by the constant flow of clean water. When the flow is considerably less, a biofilter *is* required in each tank, and the setup is instead called an automatic water change system. It still keeps the water very clean, but the water exchange is too slow to keep up with ammonia.

So, yes, it is possible to avoid cycling completely, but unless you have a flow-through system, cycling is mandatory.

How High Can Nitrate Go After Cycling?

It is clear that some nitrate can accumulate in the aquarium without harming the fish. The disagreement comes when you consider just how much can accumulate safely. The decision should take into account the fact that although we can test for nitrate, many other substances such as trace metabolites, pheromones, and pollutants build up in aquarium water. We cannot test for these and they are concentrated by evaporation.

Nitrate levels, therefore, are an indicator of the overall quality of the water, but they are only one component. The ideal nitrate level is zero. Although that is rarely attainable, it is possible to keep the level quite low with regular large water changes. You goal should be to keep it as low as you can, which will also keep down the level of other pollutants that you cannot test for. There is no such thing as too much water changing, either in volume or in frequency. Fish will thrive with 100-percent daily changes.

What about "Fishless Cycling"?

You can grow a biofilter without using fish in the tank to provide the ammonia to feed the system. Since there are no fish living in the tank, you can let ammonia and nitrite levels

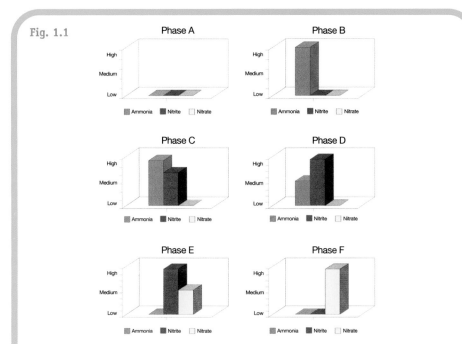

Fig. 1.1

Cycling can be broken down into six basic phases (A-F). In phase A, all nitrogen levels are at zero. Phase B is indicated by a sharp rise in Ammonia (blue). In phase C, the ammonia level is still high as the nitrite (red) level rises, too. Phase D shows the ammonia level beginning to drop as the nitrite level climbs still higher. Phase E can be identified when the ammonia level has fallen close to zero, the nitrite level begins to drop, and the nitrate (yellow) level begins to rise. Finally, in phase F we see a marked decrease in both ammonia and nitrite while the nitrate level tests in moderate to high levels.

skyrocket, which greatly speeds up the process of cycling. So, how do you feed the bacteria?

You can use ammonia. Common household ammonia often contains perfumes, detergent, or other harmful substances, but if you can find pure ammonia solution, you can use that, about a capful. Or you can use a bit of ammonium chloride powder. When your daily tests indicate the ammonia level has dropped, add more. That should also signal you to try testing for nitrite. If there is no measurable nitrite, add the ammonia and test for nitrite again the next time the ammonia drops.

Ironically, you can also use fish for fishless cycling. A chunk of fresh or frozen fish flesh, added to the tank, will decompose, producing plenty of ammonia to feed the bacteria.

Chapter 2

My Tank's Water Problems Solved!

Since an aquarium is filled mostly with water, problems with the water are among the most common difficulties an aquarist will face. In the previous chapter we dealt with cycling, which concerns several invisible toxins that can accumulate in the water. Many water problems, however, are quite visible—sometimes with strong olfactory components, too.

Why is the Water Cloudy?

Cloudy water is often the first problem a new aquarist faces, sometimes as soon as the tank is filled!

Gravel Dust

Aquarists often learn the proper way to clean new gravel only after they've produced a tank full of milky water. Natural aquarium gravel or sand is full of dust and minute particles that result both from the production of the gravel and from transport, during which abrasion of the grains against each other produces additional dust.

The best way to clean all this from the gravel is to start before you put the gravel in the tank. Place it in a large bucket or tub outdoors. Take a garden hose and fill the container, stirring the gravel well. Occasionally dump off most of the water, but keep stirring the gravel. When the water running out of the container is clear, the gravel is clean.

If this must be done inside, you can use a smaller container set in the sink and do part of the gravel at a time. Position the container right under the faucet, and stir the gravel as the water flows.

Some aquarium gravel is sealed with an epoxy coating on each grain. This gravel will contain little

if any dust, and it only needs a brief rinse before being placed into the aquarium. Read the manufacturer's instructions on the label to determine what type of gravel you are using.

Some sand will continue to produce cloudy water no matter how long you keep cleaning it. Such sand is not suitable as a substrate for your aquarium, since the water will never completely clear up with that kind of sand in the tank, and any disturbance of the sand will send up new plumes of dust.

Bacterial Bloom

Assuming you've started with clean water, a cloudy tank a day or two later is generally the result of a population explosion of microscopic life. Too small to be seen individually, the microbes are so numerous that the water takes on a cloudy appearance to the human eye. Sometimes a green algae bloom begins as a cloudy white murkiness,

Keep rinsing the gravel until the water runs clear.

In any event, the population will crash as soon as the food supply is depleted. If there is a major problem, such as the filter malfunctioning or a large dead fish decomposing in the tank, the water conditions may continue to deteriorate for a very long time before the food supply is used up. So, the first step is to determine the cause of the cloudiness and fix that. If it is just initial bacterial bloom in a new tank, it should clear up within a couple of days. A water change or two will help it along, as will a micron filter, which is a filter that removes very small particles from the aquarium water.

Gently push the gravel or sand from the rinsing vessel into place in the aquarium. Arrange it to your liking.

but dense milk-like clouding is from huge numbers of bacteria in the water. Such blooms can be followed by population explosions in various other microorganisms like paramecia and amoebae that feed on the bacteria. Without a microscope, it is impossible to see the difference, though in bright light someone with excellent eyesight can sometimes see tiny specks moving through the water. These are the tip of the microscopic iceberg; under magnification you would see swarms of different creatures.

Why is the Water Yellow?

Aquarium water can turn yellow so gradually that you don't notice it until it is quite tinted. If you hold a piece of white paper behind the aquarium and look through the water from the front, you may be surprised by how yellow the water actually is.

A yellow color can come from driftwood, especially new driftwood. Wood leaches tannins and other substances into the water than can tint it quite yellow. It can take many months for most of the tannins to leach out. Other things can also tint the water, like dead or dying plants. The most common cause, however, is urine.

That's right, fish urine turns the water yellow. Depending on the size and number of the fish, this can happen rather quickly. Many people will recommend using carbon in your filter to eliminate the yellow color, but I do not.

Oh, sure, it will remove the color, but that's the problem! If you were swimming in water tinted yellow by urine, would you just want some carbon to remove the color? No, you'd want the water removed and replaced with clean water! Well, do you think your fish feel any differently? Carbon does not remove all noxious substances, but by removing the tint, it fools you into thinking the water is clean.

The best cure, absolutely, for yellow water is a large water change—actually, large water changes made on a regular basis, since these will prevent the problem from ever occurring in the first place.

Yuck, Pea Soup!

Green water is not a very common problem, but it is very frustrating when

Gradual Stability

The stability of the water in an aquarium depends on many factors, some of them biological, so it can take some time for a new setup to stabilize.

it occurs. It starts as a green tint but can quickly become so densely green that you cannot see anything at all in the tank, unless a fish comes right up to the glass.

The green in the water is algae, specifically single-celled critters that float or swim around in the water. A wide variety of organisms can create green water, but they all share the fact that they are photosynthetic, like plants. Thus, they require nutrients and light to grow. A tank near a window may have a chronic problem with algae of all kinds.

Is It Dangerous?

An algae bloom is not in itself dangerous (unless it is caused by certain cyanobacteria, like the infamous red tide, which does not happen in aquariums), but it can be harmful to your fish in indirect ways.

First, since oxygen production

during photosynthesis ceases in the dark, the algae will compete with your fish for oxygen at night. Depending on the number of fish and the density of the algae, this could be a problem. Second, if you take steps to kill the algae, the decomposition of all those millions of microorganisms can overwhelm your biofilter and kill your fish—the equivalent of dumping several handfuls of dead plants or a few dead fish into your tank.

If you are struggling with green water, you may be amazed to find that some aquarists try to produce it intentionally. The microscopic organisms that live in green water are excellent food for many newly hatched fish. Green water is also one of the best foods for live food organisms like rotifers and daphnia, which some aquarists culture to feed them to their fish.

Ironically, although green water can be persistent and hard to combat, it is often difficult to grow it on purpose. Obviously, a precise combination of factors is necessary. When those factors are present, however, it will grow with a fury.

How Do I Fix It?

A major water change (90 to 100 percent) will instantly clear the water, of course, but it will not prevent a recurrence. Keeping the light off on the aquarium will starve out algae, so if you turn off the lights after the water change, it will help. At the same

Fight the Cause, Not the Result

It is tempting to focus on symptoms like green water, but eliminating symptoms may not do anything to solve the cause of the problem, and the symptoms will just return.

time, evaluate your feeding regimen and determine if you are overfeeding, which can lead to the elevated nutrient levels that algae thrive on. In an aquarium, as opposed to an outdoor pond, it is very easy to control the amount of light the tank receives, and algae cannot grow without light.

It is very important, however, to figure out the source of the excess nutrients. Clean the filter, vacuum the gravel, and check for detritus in back corners or a dead fish among the rocks. It may help to think in reverse of the way people who want to culture green water do. They often use dirty aquarium water and place the container in full sun or under bright lights.

It is not a good idea to use chemicals to kill the algae. Aside from the negative impact this can have on your biofilter, chemicals present two familiar problems: They do nothing to remove the cause, and add a massive bioload to your tank in terms of all the algae they kill.

Is That an Oil Slick?

You may find a film on the top of your tank that looks like a miniature oil slick. Most of the time, that is exactly what it is—an oil slick! It doesn't take much oil to form a film over the entire surface; since the film is so thin, even a single drop of oil can cover a medium-sized tank's surface. The oil may come from the air in your home, which can contain aerosol droplets of oil from a variety of sources, including cooking. Or, it may have been brought into the tank on your hands, or through a faulty air pump, or even from something you

fed your fish.

If the oil is from cooking or from fish food, it may eventually be consumed by bacteria in the tank. If it is not an animal or vegetable oil, if it is some sort of lubricating or petroleum oil, it may not be biodegradable, and bacteria will not eat it.

Often such a film of oil is noticed only when the normal water movement in the tank stops. Small amounts of oil will be unable to form a solid film in the presence of currents strong enough to break up the film, but if the water movement ceases, or if there is

Live plants will compete with less-desirable algae for available nutrients.

you should look for the cause and eliminate it.

It is important not to stick your hands into your aquarium if you have soap residue, lotions, perfumes, or other chemicals on your skin. Aside from possibly producing oil slicks, these can harm your fish or kill them outright.

What is this Foam?

Sometimes a foam similar to soap suds will appear at the water surface, especially in corners or along a glass side and particularly when the water has been agitated vigorously. Assuming you have not gotten soap or detergent into the water, which can itself have tragic consequences, such foam is normally a protein scum. You can also

sufficient oil, once a complete film forms over the entire water surface, it can effectively block gas exchange.

This suggests a quick fix: increase the water movement to break up the oil slick. Or, you can go the other way: turn off all filters and pumps and let the water become still. Then float a paper towel on the water surface and remove it. If necessary, take another towel and repeat the process until the oil is gone.

An occasional bit of oil is not a reason for concern, but if the slick recurs frequently, or if it is very heavy,

The Quick Cure-All

Remember that massive water changes can cure just about anything that is wrong with your aquarium water. In many cases they also help eliminate the cause of the problem. At the very least, they protect your fish from harm while you fix what is wrong.

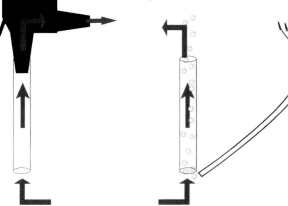

Fig. 2.1

Powerheads or air can be utilized to increase water flow in your aquarium, thus preventing excess alage from growing in your tank.

observe foam under natural conditions at the seashore or in a bubbling stream. When waves drive water against pier pilings, for example, or when flowing water bounces off rocks in a brook, air is incorporated, and dissolved proteins and other surfactants churn into a foam.

This tendency of many dissolved substances to coat air bubbles, creating a foam, is exploited in devices called protein skimmers, which are widely used in saltwater aquariums to remove wastes and other pollutants. In a simple freshwater system, the presence of this type of foam is a signal to clean things up. Clean the filter media, do a thorough gravel vacuuming while changing some of the water, and check for problems like an unnoticed dead fish or pile of uneaten food.

Do not mistake a betta's or gourami's bubblenest for a protein foam! If the foam is composed of tiny bubbles piled tightly together and covers only a small area, check to see if a male labyrinth fish is hanging out underneath, challenging any other fish that comes close. There doesn't have to be a female in the tank for a male to build a nest, as in the wild he will not try to attract a mate until he has a nest to show off.

Why Is My Tank's Water too Hot or too Cold?

Assuming that your heater is functioning properly, that it is not stuck in either the on or off position, and does heat up when the indicator light is on, there are various reasons why it is unable to maintain the tank at the proper temperature.

Remember that a heater should never be removed from the water while it is still plugged in. The tube can overheat very quickly. It can cause serious burns or start a fire, and if a glass tube gets wet after it has heated up, the glass will break.

Area versus Volume

Before we look at heater problems, it is important to understand that smaller tanks will heat up or cool off much more quickly than larger ones. You know this intuitively if you think in terms of a cup of hot coffee versus a

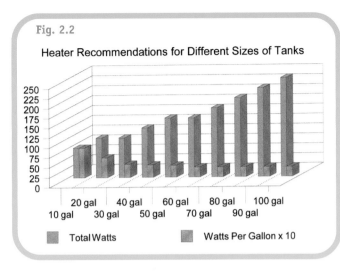

Fig. 2.2

Heater Recommendations for Different Sizes of Tanks

(bar chart with y-axis values: 250, 225, 200, 175, 150, 125, 100, 75, 50, 25, 0; x-axis labels: 10 gal, 20 gal, 30 gal, 40 gal, 50 gal, 60 gal, 70 gal, 80 gal, 90 gal, 100 gal)

■ Total Watts   ■ Watts Per Gallon x 10

tanks need correspondingly more or less wattage per gallon. See Fig. 2.2.

Other than volume, the temperature range of the room in which the aquarium is located will affect how much wattage you need to keep the aquarium at the proper temperature.

freshly drawn hot bath. If you leave for a short phone call, your coffee may well be cold when you return, but your tub will still be warm and inviting.

This is because small volumes have a relatively greater surface area than large ones. Surface area (the outside of a container) is how heat gets out of the container, but volume (the space inside the container) is what holds heat.

A smaller aquarium has relatively more surface area than a large aquarium, so it will cool off much faster. You can think of this in terms of all the heat in the smaller aquarium being closer to a surface than in the larger tank.

So, a 20-gallon (75-liter) aquarium usually needs a 100-watt heater, but a 100-gallon (380-liter) tank will probably only need a 300-watt unit—three times the heating power for five times the water. Much smaller or much larger

Too Cool

If you lower the normal temperature in the room in which your aquarium is located, a heater that was adequate may no longer be able to keep up with the task. Likewise, an aquarium that was set up in warm weather may start cooling off when winter arrives. If the heater has too little wattage for the setup, the heater can lose out to the room temperature. If the heater remains on all the time, and the tube gets hot, but the tank is too cool, then you need more wattage—either add a heater or replace the current one with a more powerful one.

Too Warm

If an aquarium is too warm but the heater is not stuck, there must be some other heat source. The most common culprit is the aquarium lighting, especially on smaller tanks, which heat

Different Volume Tanks
With The Same Surface Areas

The aquariums below both have the same surface area, but hold far different volumes of water. However, each can hold almost the same amount of biomass. Surface area, not total tank volume, determines the amount of biomass an aquarium can support.

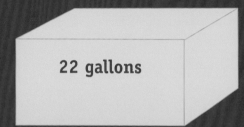

22 gallons

Total Cubic Area
3 x 3 x 1 = 3 ft³

Surface Area
3 x 1 = 3 ft²

67 gallons

Total Cubic Area
3 x 1 x 3 = 9 ft³

Surface Area
3 x 1 = 3 ft²

up much more quickly than large tanks. Remember that an aquarium will not be cooler than the room. If the location of the aquarium is too hot, then the water will be, too.

Too Much Variation

If the temperature of your aquarium varies more than a degree or two, first seek to identify an external cause. The most obvious would be if the temperature of the room in which the tank is located varies a great deal, perhaps because you turn the heat down substantially at night or when you are not home. In this case, you need a more powerful heater to keep up the temperature when the room gets cold.

Location Concerns

The positioning of your aquarium can affect its stability. Avoid areas of temperature extremes near doors, windows, or heating or air conditioning vents. Avoid direct sunlight as well.

If the temperature swings up too high while the heater is on, but only drops to the proper temperature just before the heater comes back on, your heater is too powerful for the size tank you have. In such a case, although the heater shuts off when the set temperature is reached, the element is still hot, and it continues to radiate heat into the water, causing it to rise above the set temperature. This effect is minimal with the proper heater, but a grossly oversized one will heat the water significantly even after turning off.

SMALL FRY

Looking Without Touching

An aquarium is a tempting target for inquisitive minds and fingers. Teaching your child to enjoy the aquarium without touching it or its support equipment will protect your fish as well as your child. It will also serve as an important lesson in self-restraint and patience.

29

My Tank's Water Problems Solved!

Chapter **3**

Other Tank Problems Solved!

Now that we've discussed problems with the water conditions in your aquarium, let's take a look at the most common problems new aquarists run into in terms of things—other than water—inside their tanks.

any of these problems involve the growth of various organisms that feed on the excess nutrients in the tank, most often nitrates and phosphates. These nutrients, even in excess, are relatively nontoxic accumulations as a result of normal biological processes that take place in all aquariums. They are typically the same nutrients that aquatic plants use, and in heavily planted tanks the idea is to get the plants to out-compete the other organisms such as algae. This is not possible in a typical aquarium that contains a few clumps of plants at most, and the best way to eliminate the nutrients is simply to dilute them with frequent water changes.

Nutrient Export

You will often see "nutrient export" in hobbyist literature. This refers to the removal of excess nutrients from the aquarium, using any means. Water change is a means of nutrient export,

Vallisneria is a common and easy-to-keep plant that will effectively reduce nutrients in your tank.

The Glass Box Ecosystem

It is much easier to achieve balance than absolute control in your aquarium. Letting some algae grow can prevent less desirable types from growing.

but so is scraping algae off the glass. Algae use up nutrients to grow their cells; when you remove the algae, you remove the nutrients.

Common Algae

Sometimes an aquarist chooses one type of algal growth over another that is either less desirable or harder to control. "Plain algae," the green film that grows on just about any tank glass, is usually the most desirable, and it is easy to control by periodic scraping. Not only does this function as a nutrient export, but it suppresses undesirable algal growth by using up all the nutrients before the other algae can get a start. Keep in mind that living systems are much easier to balance than to control.

Eew! What Is This Slime?

A common problem is slime covering everything in the tank—gravel, rocks, plants, ornaments, even the glass walls. The velvety coating can be green, blue, red, or brown. In most cases these slimes are composed of humongous colonies of single-celled cyanobacteria,

also known as blue-green algae. Under bright lighting the slimy mat may be dotted with bubbles; this is oxygen being produced through photosynthesis and bubbling into the water.

A cyanobacterial blanket, though rather thick, is usually simply draped over the objects in the aquarium; it is not attached to them. Thus, you can easily siphon it out. The suction from your gravel tube may not be sufficient to dislodge it, but if you remove the tube and use only the siphon hose, it should suck it right up. This, of course, removes the slime, but it doesn't eliminate the cause, which is an excess of nutrients.

Brown Algae

A brown growth primarily on the aquarium glass is usually from different single-celled algae, either diatoms or dinoflagellates. These typically appear under low lighting conditions. With more light, they are usually replaced by either cyanobacteria or true algae.

Aside from being unsightly, algae can kill plants by smothering them and blocking the light from reaching their leaves. They also can give the aquarium a very strong organic odor, and in rare cases can release toxins that will harm your fish.

The Fix?

It is possible to kill cyanobacteria with antibiotics. This is definitely not a good idea, since antibiotics are indiscriminant in the bacteria that they kill and they can kill off your biofilter, which will create a dangerous situation. One of the biggest problems, however, is that they do kill the cyanobacteria! Not only have you not addressed the cause of the outbreak, you have now added a whole bunch of dead cyanobacteria to the bioload of the tank, perhaps enough to overwhelm the surviving biofilter, and certainly sufficient to fuel an even bigger outbreak of cyanobacteria once the antibiotic degrades.

Siphoning out the slime and doing a thorough gravel vacuuming and water change is the best approach. Repeat as necessary, and soon the problem should disappear. Cyanobacteria are common in a new setup that is still approaching equilibrium but do not usually plague a mature aquarium.

Help! There's Algae Everywhere!

When the green covering over everything is less soft and velvety and more rigid, it is green algae. While cyanobacteria film can be lifted off in sheets, algae must be scraped off. Before we talk about eliminating this type of algae, we should consider whether that is a good idea, remembering what we discussed above about nutrient export.

First of all, it is practically impossible to remove all algae in an aquarium. A stable aquarium usually has some algae growing on surfaces. In an extremely heavily planted tank, the plants may use up all the nutrients, effectively starving out algae, but even such an aquarium can need the help of some algae-eating fish or invertebrates to keep everything clean.

In all other tanks, you should consider letting algae grow on the glass panes that are not used for viewing—usually the back and often one or both ends. By keeping only the front viewing panel scraped clean of algae, you accomplish several things besides saving yourself work.

Many fish love grazing on algae. When you see them picking away at the green on the glass, they are getting

Plecos will remove algae from glass and other surfaces.

The Siamese flying fox is an accomplished algae destroyer!

strands growing in profusion on rocks, plants, and other surfaces. Many fish will eat it, and it is simple to remove. Simply snag it on a rough stick or twirl it to wrap it around an old toothbrush and then pull the whole clump free.

As with any algae, removing excess nutrients and controlling the lighting will help prevent an outbreak, or treat one if it occurs.

a lot more than just algae. An algal mat is a microhabitat that supports an enormous variety of tiny invertebrates, all of which are tasty snacks for your fish.

In addition, if several panes of the aquarium are algae meadows, any excess nutrients in the water will be used up by them; this makes it less likely that algae will grow where you do not want it—on ornaments or live plants.

When you do scrape algae off the glass, do it before a water change, and try to vacuum out all the algae as you siphon out the water. Until the algae are removed from the tank, you have simply moved them from one place to another, and there was no nutrient export.

Yuck, Green Hair!

Hair algae can plague planted tanks. It is as you'd expect—green hair-like

Now Black Fur?

Beard or brush algae growth starts out as tiny dark puffs appearing on surfaces throughout the tank. Actually a red algae, this appears very dark, almost black. They quickly grow into a blue-gray-looking "fur" that can be an inch (2.5 cm) or so long that ripples in the water current. It can quickly cover everything in the tank, though it tends not to grow on the substrate, and it is not always successful establishing itself on living plant leaves.

The effect of this can be eerily beautiful—it gives a tank almost a haunted look. Most aquarists, however, consider it an unsightly scourge, and aquatic gardeners loathe finding it in their planted tanks.

Other Tank Problems Solved!

The Fix?

There are fish that eat black algae, but almost all of them are fish you probably don't want in your aquarium. In addition, fish that will eat it often prefer the food you feed their tankmates, and they won't eat the algae unless you starve them. Three animals that are used with considerable success to control beard algae are the Siamese algae eater, *Crossocheilus siamensis*, a difficult-to-find fish that has several look-alikes that do not eat black algae; the Amano shrimp, *Caridina japonica*; and the American flagfish, *Jordanella floridae*.

You can kill black algae chemically, but this is drastic and fraught with side effects. It also does nothing to remove the cause of the infestation or to prevent its recurrence. The best weapons are:

- Increasing water flow. Beard algae prefer calm waters.

- Increasing lighting. Green algae and higher plants can out-compete the black algae with sufficient light.

- Removing excess nutrients. Step up your water changes to remove the nutrients which the algae use.

Yikes! Worms!

Occasionally an aquarium will experience a population explosion of tiny white or light brown worms, about one-eighth of an inch long, (2.5 cm) crawling all over, including on the glass. These are most likely planarians, flatworms like the ones used in biology classes for regeneration experiments.

The planarians are introduced into your aquarium on plants or with fish, but a tiny population will never be noticed. They show up when an aquarium is overfed, especially with fresh meat. With a sufficient supply of food, the planarians can multiply quickly into gigantic populations.

If faced with a planarian infestation, a quick fix is to immediately get out your siphon and change most of the tank's water, vacuuming the gravel several times and sucking up as many of the worms as you can. Chances are that

Otto cats are perfect algae eaters for small aquariums.

The Chinese algae eater may get too big, and too aggressive, for most hobbyist's tanks.

a lot of filth will get flushed out of the gravel as you vacuum it.

If a couple days later the worms are back in force, repeat the whole procedure, making sure to push the gravel tube all the way to the bottom of the tank to stir up the substrate and siphon out all the accumulated garbage.

Again, avoid the temptation to reach for a chemical cure. Many compounds, especially copper solutions, will kill planarians. By now you know the "but" that comes next: they can also kill off your biofilter, they do nothing to remove the cause of the infestation, and they add to the problem with all the decomposing critters you killed.

To prevent a reinfestation, you need to alter your feeding habits. A properly maintained aquarium cannot sustain many planarians. Once the tank is clean and the worms are eliminated, make sure you do not overfeed and vacuum the gravel at least once a week to keep

a flatworm food source from accumulating.

They've Got TENTACLES!

If you've got good eyes, you might notice tiny animals that look like a thick stalk topped with waving tentacles. They are fairly transparent, but they can be colored brown or green. These are hydra, which are tiny relatives of marine corals and sea anemones. These invertebrates are usually only a problem in fry tanks. This is because they can trap very tiny fish in their tentacles, kill them, and eat them. It is also because one of the best foods for hydra is baby brine shrimp, and the shrimp are often fed in great numbers to baby fish. Unfortunately, then, the fry's food also feeds the little predators. They can be present in small numbers in any tank and go unnoticed. If baby brine shrimp are fed in quantity, the hydra can undergo a population explosion and become a visible infestation.

A few fish, like the blue gourami, will eat hydra. Since, however, hydra are only a concern in tank with very small fish, any fish that will eat the hydra will also be able to eat the other fish! Fortunately, they are not a common problem and can be tolerated in small numbers. In fact, they are present undetected in many setups and can be considered a fascinating part of an aquarium ecosystem.

Pee-yoo! What is That Smell?

An aquarium normally has a very mild, pleasant, earthy odor. On occasion a tank will become quite rank, smelling more like a swamp—or worse! There may be the odor of rotten eggs, and bubbles may be seen in the gravel, occasionally rising to the surface. In addition, the gravel may develop black patches. What's wrong? The answer, unfortunately, is putrefaction.

Putrefaction

This term means roughly "making putrid," and it refers to various processes of anaerobic decomposition—the breakdown of organic matter in an environment without oxygen. It is the inevitable result of gross overfeeding, often accompanied by gross overcrowding of the fish. The uneaten food falls into the

Cause & Effect

Many aspects of aquarium maintenance teach a child cause and effect, the knowledge of which is the basis of responsibility. Leave the light on too much, algae will grow. Hit the glass, and it will crack. Overfeed the fish, and they will die. Letting your child help take care of the tank will be a powerful learning tool.

gravel, where bacteria feed on it, quickly using up all the available oxygen. At this point anaerobic bacteria, which live in oxygen-less environments, proliferate. They produce hydrogen sulfide (which smells like rotten eggs) and other nasty substances.

The reason the tank starts to stink is that the gases are escaping from the gravel bed. This also means that the gases are dissolving into the tank water, and as many of them are quite toxic, this is a real danger for your fish.

Prompt action is necessary. If possible, remove all the fish to another tank, using water from their aquarium. Take care not to disturb the gravel as you work. This will save your fish from the worst of it. If you cannot remove the fish, you will have to work around them, but they may not all survive.

Snails may quickly become a nuisance in your aquarium.

After you remove the fish, drain out all the water, take the aquarium outside, and dump the gravel. The gravel can be washed and bleached, but it will take a long time to eliminate the smell, and the black stain may remain anyway. It's better to toss the gravel and get new gravel. Use a garden hose to clean out the tank thoroughly. You can now set up the aquarium again, this time being careful not to overfeed.

If you have to work with the fish still in the tank, you still must get that putrid gravel out of there. Use a large-diameter hose to siphon out all of the gravel and most of the water. (You may wish to use nose plugs!) Chances are that by now your fish are swimming in a few inches of very smelly, blue-black water. Finish draining what water is left in the tank, leaving just enough to cover the fish on the bottom.

Now, gradually refill the tank with water of the correct temperature. The reason you need to do this gradually is that your fish are under enormous stress. Their water is polluted, and they need clean water badly, but clean water

is so different chemically that they can receive a deadly shock if they are plunged too quickly into it.

Snails, Snails, Snails!

While many aquarists purchase and care for apple or mystery snails, the common pond snail and the ramshorn snail can show up on their own and quickly blanket the aquarium with their descendants.

Tiny snails or their gelatinous egg masses can arrive unnoticed with plants or fish added to the tank. They are very prolific and can soon number in the hundreds or even thousands in very large aquariums.

Snails in themselves are not bad. Many aquarists like having them around. They clean up any uneaten food or dying plants—they even eat algae! Snails are also interesting aquarium inhabitants. On the negative side, since they are additional animals, they increase the bioload of the tank. In reality, though, few snails can compete with fish for food, so if you have a profusion of the shelled creatures, you are probably feeding more food than your fish can eat. In this case, it's preferable to have the wastes of the snails than the decomposing uneaten food. Some hobbyists, however, don't want them around, and even those who do sometimes realize they have too many. So, what can you do about them? That depends on whether you want to keep down their numbers or get rid of them completely.

Control

Simply cutting back on feeding your fish will slow down the increase in the snail population, but it will not reduce their existing numbers. Fortunately, you can remove excess snails from an aquarium very easily. Put a piece of lettuce or a small dish with a few pellets of fish food in it on the gravel when you turn out the lights. In the morning, simply remove the lettuce or the dish, which should be covered with snails. You can also use a net to sweep them off the aquarium glass.

To drastically reduce their numbers, add a few snail eating loaches to the tank. Yo-yo or clown loaches are the most popular, but any should do the trick. These fish are best kept in schools of at least three to six, and they will make quick work of the snails, sucking them right out of their shells for a snack of escargot sushi. If you do not want the loaches in the tank permanently, make sure you leave them for a few weeks after you no longer see any snails so that any snail eggs that remain can hatch out.

It is most often the case that the fish will completely eliminate the snails, but sometimes when the loaches are realize they have them until one night they shine a flashlight on their tank and see hundreds of them everywhere.

Elimination

The only safe way to completely eliminate snails is to tear down the tank and soak the filter, the gravel, and all ornaments in a concentrated salt solution or in a dilute bleach solution. Living plants must be disposed of. After all of this, all it will take is one snail egg mass on a plant to start the whole thing over again. So, if you are determined to remain snail-free, new plants must be treated chemically to kill snail eggs. In most cases it's hardly worth the bother.

The yo-yo loach is an effective snail hunter. Clown loaches also prey on snails.

removed from the tank, the snails will reappear. Since most snails are hermaphrodites (having both male and female organs), it only takes one cautious snail hiding somewhere in the tank to repopulate it.

This post-loach phenomenon can happen with any type of snails, but it is most common with the Malaysian trumpet snail, a long, conical snail that lives in the gravel. These snails are nocturnal, spending the day deep in the gravel, and many aquarists never

I've Sprung a Leak!

Aquarium leaks are caused either by cracks in the glass or plastic or by failures in the silicone seal. They range in severity from a slight drip to a complete disaster with all of the water, gravel, and fish on the living room floor—or dripping through your downstairs neighbor's ceiling.

Do not underestimate the weight of water, or the explosive effect that damage to a tank can cause. A 55-

gallon tank (210 l) contains about 400 pounds (182 kg) of water, held in place by glass and sealant; if either fails, a mighty heavy wave will sweep through the room.

Cracks

While a hard blow to an aquarium from the outside can certainly crack it, many tanks are cracked by the inhabitants. Very large fish, like some cichlids and catfishes, have been known to spook and bolt into the side of an aquarium hard enough to break the glass. Usually if the fish is being kept in a sufficiently large tank, the glass will be thick enough to handle such collisions. Most cases of breakage occur in circumstances such as an 18-in. (45 cm) fish being kept in a 55-gallon (210-liter) aquarium, but given enough motivation to escape, any large fish can break glass of considerable thickness.

Rather small fish can also crack aquarium glass. Fish which dig, burrow, or otherwise excavate can undermine

Emergency Housing

Fish can be housed temporarily in a plastic, glass, or stainless steel container. Remember, though, that without a biofilter, you will have to change the water a few times a day to prevent ammonia buildup. All emergency housing is best thought of as temporary housing, and the fish should only be in such containers for a few days at the most.

large rocks, which then fall either against the glass side or onto the glass bottom. Again cichlids are often involved in such destruction, but any fish whose activities upset a rockpile can cause a disaster.

To prevent such tragedies, place rock formations directly on the bottom glass and fill the gravel in around them. Also, make sure the rocks are well balanced and sturdy. An added security measure is to use aquarium sealant to glue the rocks together before they get wet.

Obtain two pieces of glass larger than the crack, and silicone one over the crack on the inside of the tank and the other over the crack on the outside. Wait 48 hours before testing the tank by filling it.

Balancing Act

An aquarium setup weighs approximately 10 pounds per gallon (more than a kilo per liter) due to the weight of the tank, gravel, rocks, plus the water. Never place an aquarium on anything other than a stand specifically made to hold that kind of massive weight.

On the Level

Sealant Failures

Modern aquarium silicone sealers are so good that they almost never fail just from use or age. The bond is, however, easily broken by excessive stress forces. There are numerous ways in which a sealant bond can be stressed.

While aquarium sealant has enormous holding power, sheer forces can break the seal. These result when unequal stresses are applied to different sections of the tank. If the aquarium is not level, the pressure at various points will differ. If the surface on which the tank rests is not flat, one corner will be uphill from another, and the bending forces can rip the seal.

Stress Fractures

When the bottom glass of an aquarium breaks, it is often because the tank is not on a level surface. If the sealant holds despite the strain, the glass may not. Since glass is not very flexible, it will crack.

Prevention

Before you put any water into an aquarium, use a level to check that is it level both right-to-left and front-to-back. Check the surface is its resting on to be sure it is level and smooth. Even minor imperfections can cause a tank to leak or crack. Many people place a piece of foam board under an aquarium, especially if it is a large one. This soft base will conform to the contours below it and can even out small irregularities.

Always make sure that your aquarium is level before filling it with water.

43

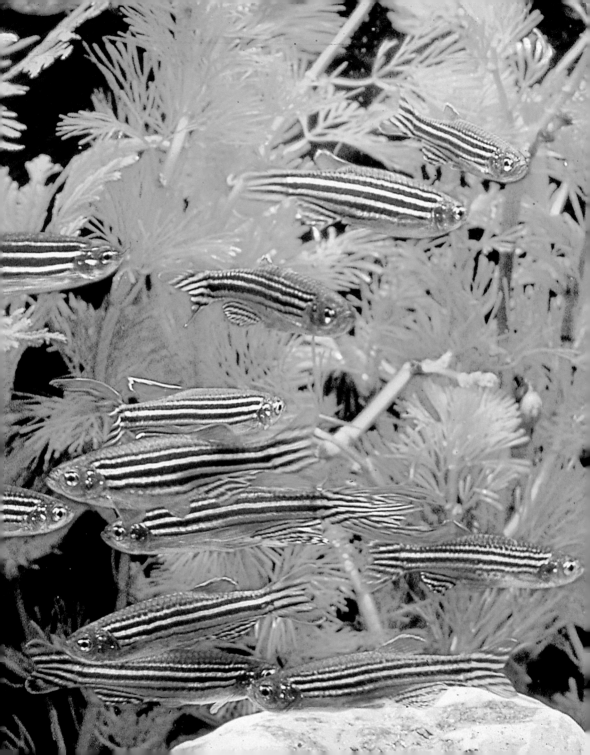

Chapter 4

Fish Illnesses Solved!

There are several ways to tell if a fish is sick or not, and with a little experience, you will be able to notice the telltale signs of illness. This is one reason why it is important to watch your fish. By knowing how they normally look and behave, you will be able to detect when they are not feeling well. In this chapter we're going to look at some of the common ailments you might face as an aquarist.

Powerheads are effective at increasing the dissolved oxygen content in aquariums.

Various behaviors should immediately indicate to you that your fish are in trouble and need help. These include gasping at the surface, showing white spots on the fins and body, having clamped fins, shimmying, and having cottony growths on their bodies.

My Fish Are Suffocating!

You find your fish all at the surface of the water, gasping laboriously. We are not talking here about a fish going to the surface for an actual breath of air. Some species, like bettas and cory cats, breathe air in addition to breathing water through their gills. They do not, however, stay at the surface gasping. That is very serious, and it indicates your fish are not getting sufficient oxygen. This is a very serious situation, roughly equivalent to a person choking and turning blue.

If only some of your fish are gasping, it may be that something is wrong with them, but it can also be that they have higher oxygen needs than your other fish, which will soon be gasping at the surface, too.

Fixing the Problem

As soon as you see fish gasping at the surface, you should start draining water out of the tank. While it drains you can try to figure out what is wrong. By then you should be ready to refill the tank, and in most cases, a quick water change is the best solution to the problem anyway. It is often not a permanent solution, however, so take the necessary steps to prevent a recurrence.

In any case, the problem may or may not be with the oxygenation of your water. Let's look at why.

How Fish Breathe

Fish breathe by passing water over their gills. They open their mouth, take in water, then pump it over the gills, the water then exits through the open gill flaps. Fish have to expend a lot of energy to breathe. While we simply pull oxygen-rich (20 percent) air into our lungs and push it back out, fish have to move oxygen-low (<.001 percent) water over their gills. Water is much denser and more viscous than air, too— imagine the difference between pushing a 5-gallon (19 l) bucket of air

It's extremely important to have a high oxygen level in aquariums that contain many fishes.

across the floor and pushing a 5-gallon (19 l) bucket of water. It gives a whole new meaning to "breathing heavily"!

So, why do they gasp at the surface? The fish are not gulping air. If you look closely, you will see that they are actually keeping their mouths just below the surface of the water. In this way, they are taking in the very topmost layer of water, which has the highest oxygen content. Oxygen only enters the water at the interface—the surface, so the top film is most oxygen rich.

Two things can bring a fish to this point: reduced oxygenation of the water and an impairment of the gills' ability to extract oxygen from the water.

Air bubbles can help raise the dissolved oxygen level in aquariums.

Low O₂ Levels

Fish can succumb very quickly to suffocation in low oxygen levels. Low oxygen levels can occur in an aquarium for many reasons:

- *Overcrowding.* When the fish oxygen requirement for all the fish is greater than the capacity of the tank's water to exchange gases, the fish will use up all the oxygen in the water faster than it can be replaced. The only solution in this case is to quickly move some of the fish to another aquarium. Increasing aeration with air stones or a powerhead can give emergency relief, but you do not want to operate a tank this close to crisis for long— what if the power fails?

- *Temperature increase.* The warmer the water, the less oxygen it can hold. If the fishs' oxygen needs are only

Fish Can Get Sick

If your fish become ill, explain to your child that they are sick, just like we get sick. Tell them what you are doing to help the fish. Since not all fish ailments are easily treated, be sure not to promise that the fish will get better.

slightly less than the tank's capacity, an increase in temperature, as during a heat wave, can suffocate the fish. Cool the tank by replacing the solid cover with screening and position a fan blowing right across the surface. This will greatly increase evaporation, which cools the tank.

- *Increased salinity.* The higher the salinity (amount of dissolved substances), the less oxygen water can hold. If you have added tonics, medications, or other chemicals to the tank, you may have reduced the oxygen-carrying capacity of the tank's water to dangerous levels. Do a large water change to dilute the dissolved substances, then make provisions to lower the stocking rate of the tank.

- *Extreme decomposition.* Dead fish, dead plants, or dead algae can cause an oxygen crash because the bacteria decomposing the organic matter use a great deal of oxygen.

All of these scenarios indicate in most cases that your tank is overstocked because if it isn't, the system should be able to carry the fish with no problems.

Impaired Gill Function

If the problem is not with the aeration of the tank water, the fish's gills must be compromised in some way. Here are the most common causes:

- *Ammonia burn.* Before it kills a fish outright, ammonia will burn delicate tissues, of which the gills are the most sensitive. If the fish is immediately placed into clean, ammonia-free water, it may recover. If severe gill damage has occurred, it will die anyway. Having an adequate biofilter will prevent this problem from ever occurring.

• *Nitrite concentration.* Before nitrite kills a fish outright, it binds with the hemoglobin in the fish's blood, which lowers its ability to carry oxygen to the fish's tissues. Having an adequate biofilter will also prevent this problem from ever occurring. In this case, there is a chance of reversing the damage, since the cause is chemical (binding to the hemoglobin) rather than physical (destroying gill tissue): add salt to the water. To know how much to add requires accurate testing of the levels of both nitrite and chloride ions in the water. Fortunately, most fish can tolerate salt quite well, so tossing a handful of aquarium salt into the tank may suffice. Even better would be to change most of the water in the tank, then add the salt. Remember this is only a temporary fix; you must then find out what is causing the nitrite concentration and remedy that situation, or your fish will just be stricken again.

• *Parasites.* Various parasites can infect the gills and impair their ability to exchange oxygen. Ich and flukes are

Just Say No

When you buy fish, check the entire tank thoroughly for sickly looking fish. Purchasing even a healthy looking fish from a tank with sick ones is a very bad risk. And, of course, only buy fish that look to be in the best of health regardless of what any fish seems to beg you to do or pet store owner may try to sell you.

the most common. Flukes are found mainly in wild-caught fish, but ich is extremely common in all aquarium fish [See the next heading, "White Spots."]. If you eliminate the infection, you eliminate the strain on the gills.

White Spots

Finding white spots on your fish—so that it looks like it's been salted—is cause for immediate concern. The most likely culprit is ich (pronounced "ick"), a protozoan infection that is highly contagious and often fatal, but which, fortunately, is rather easy to treat—if you know how. And that involves understanding the parasite's life cycle.

The white spots you see on the fish are the ich organisms embedded in the fish's flesh. They scrape away at the fish's tissue, eating fluids and bits of flesh and getting fat. You cannot attack them at this stage, as they are well protected inside their shells and the fish's skin.

When they are plump enough, they drop off the fish and hook on to some solid surface. There they stay inside their tough shells, multiplying. They are also impervious to attack at this stage of their life.

Finally they break out, and hundreds—or thousands—of the creatures swim off, looking for a fish to infect. This is the stage at which they are vulnerable, and the only time you can kill them. You should use a threefold attack:

Salt & Heat

Raising the temperature a few degrees and adding a bit of salt to the water is an appropriate treatment for almost any fish ailment. It's a safe, inexpensive, and easy course of action that often is all you need.

This ruby barb is infected with velvet, a parasitic disease.

1. Temperature

Your first method of attack is to raise the temperature. In fact, temperature alone can eliminate the infection. Raising the temperature to 90°F (32°C) for ten days will kill off the protozoans as they hatch out. Most fish can handle this, but be prepared to supplement the aeration of the tank if they seem stressed for oxygen.

As part of a different treatment, raising the temperature into the low to mid 80°F (high 20°C) shortens the time needed to eliminate the infection. The warmer the water, the faster the life cycle, and the more often the parasites will be open to attack.

2. Medication

Salt is effective against ich, but sometimes only at concentrations the fish don't tolerate well. Adding 1 to 2 tsp of salt per gallon of water is sometimes enough.

An alternative is to use any of the commercially available anti-ich preparations that usually contain copper. Follow the manufacturer's directions carefully. If you have scaleless fish like loaches, use only half the recommended dose.

To properly use medication, you would need laboratory tests to determine the causative organism, which would indicate what drug, if any, to use. In humans, a cough could indicate an allergy or tuberculosis; a fever could be from a cold or meningitis. Well, these symptoms in your fish can indicate such a wide variety of problems that there is

The Quick Cure-All

In Chapter 2, we discussed making massive water changes as a cure for just about any problem with your aquarium water. Well, it's also the best first step for just about any illness your fish might experience. What's more, it also prevents illness by keeping your fish in the best of health!

no way other than lab studies to determine what is wrong. Fortunately, the most common problem is bad water, and that is easily remedied.

3. Water Changes

Once or twice a day, remove half the water from the tank, using a gravel tube to thoroughly vacuum the bottom. This removes enormous numbers of the parasites that have dropped off the fish before they have time to hatch out hundreds of offspring. Refill with conditioned water of the appropriate temperature. If you are using medication, re-dose after the water change.

Frequent partial water changes are needed to maintain a healthy aquarium.

By the Clock

The nature of ich's life cycle makes it possible to eliminate an infection simply by staying ahead of the parasites. It takes a lot of work and it requires two tanks. They should be bare bottomed and without live plants. The procedure is quite simple:

- Every 12 hours, move the fish from one tank to the other.

- Empty the first tank, rinse it (and any plastic plants you might be using as shelter for the fish) with a dilute bleach solution, then rinse them very well with warm water.

- Refill the tank and keep it ready for your next eradicating move.

- Continue the procedure until you have seen no spots on any of the fish for at least 24 hours.

The reason this works, of course, is that the parasites must have free-floating time off the fish to multiply before releasing the next generation that seeks out fish to infect. If you move the fish every 12 hours, the parasites do not have time to release the next generation, and they get flushed down the drain when the tank is cleaned. Each batch of parasites that drops off the fish winds up down the drain before they can reinfest the fish. This method will fail if you do not keep up with the moves, since allowing just one batch of parasites to multiply and reinfest the fish starts everything all over again.

Fish infected with ich look like they have been salted.

What Next?

There are two schools of thought regarding ich and its ability to stay dormant in an aquarium. Some argue that it is always around, and if the fish get chilled or otherwise stressed, they become susceptible. This certainly does happen; fish are stressed, ich breaks out. No new fish have been added, so there is no new source for ich.

The other argument is that since ich parasites must find a host within a couple days, if they are all killed off, there will be none left in tank. If a new fish is added, carrying ich on its body, even just one parasite, it can start an epidemic, infecting all the fish. This also does happen—very often.

So, which is it? Can ich parasites remain dormant in a tank, or do they need a living host within three days, or die? If the first it true, how come adding a new fish often results in the whole tank coming down with ich? And if the second is true, how do fish come down with ich after being stressed, when no new fish have been added?

One possible explanation is immunity. There is evidence that an infection of ich bestows some immunity on a fish that recovers. Perhaps once fish get over a particular strain of ich, they are mostly immune

Unusual behavior, like cowering in corners, is a sign that something is wrong with your fish.

to it. A few parasites might be able to feed long enough to drop off and multiply into a few free-swimming forms, and an extremely low-level infection continues—with only a spot or two on one fish at any one time. Stress the fish, and it lowers their resistance, and the disease returns in full. Likewise, add a new fish with a different strain of ich, and the whole tank succumbs to it.

This is speculation, but it accounts for the two types of observed experiences, which each seems otherwise to disqualify the other.

Clamped Fins & Shimmying

Sometimes sick fish just lie around with their fins closed up against the body, or they may clamp their fins and shimmy—swim in place. A rough analogy would be that these behaviors are similar to gross indicators of illness in humans, like fever, runny nose, shivering, coughing. You know something is wrong, but you don't know what. The difference here is that these behaviors do not indicate a mild problem in fish, but a serious one.

If many (or all) of your fish are affected, treat the whole tank. If it is only one or two fish, you should remove them to a hospital tank, but keep an eye on the others in case they also become ill.

The very first thing to check is the temperature. If it is too low, raise it. The next thing to do is make a major water

change. If these symptoms are indicative of an infection, the fresh water will lessen the stresses on your fish and at least make them feel better. These symptoms, however, usually indicate poor water conditions, and the water change will remedy that.

This water change should be about 90 percent of the aquarium's water. Drain it down to a depth of only an inch or so, and refill with conditioned water of the same temperature. In most cases this will be enough to bring the fish around. If it does not, do another water change about 12 hours later. This can be repeated as often as needed. In fact, a daily 90-percent change is the best medicine for any problem your fish might face, and it's a great tonic to keep them healthy, too!

Cottony Growths

Although usually labeled "fungus," white fuzzy patches on a fish are often a sign of bacterial infections, not fungal ones. Both, however, respond to a salt bath. Make up a small container of water using a commercial marine aquarium salt mix. Make sure it is the same temperature as the water in the aquarium in which the fish is maintained.

therapies. If the fish does not begin to get better in a few days, you will have to get a medication from your dealer. Always follow the printed instructions carefully.

Quick, First Aid!

Fish are susceptible to wounds and injuries. Blunt trauma can produce bruises, while encounters with sharp objects can cause cuts. In addition, fins can become frayed or torn. Usually these things heal up quickly, but secondary infection by bacteria or by fungi can be serious.

While you watch the fish to make sure it doesn't develop infections, you can raise the temperature a bit and add a little salt. The salt increases the fish's slime coat, which helps ward off infection and speed healing.

This koi is showing signs of a bacterial infection. Viral infections are sometimes encountered on fishes. In this case, the fish is infected with Lymphocystis.

Bad News

There are a few symptoms which indicate things that are basically not treatable. Isolation in a hospital tank with warm water and a little salt cannot hurt, and on rare occasion the fish may recover, but not often.

Once a day, place the affected fish into the bath for about 60 seconds, then remove it. Raising the temperature of the hospital tank a few degrees and adding a teaspoon of salt per gallon are good supplemental

Swimming Problems

Sometimes a fish will be unable to control its swimming. It may be upside down or just tilted at an odd angle and unable to right itself. Often attributed to nebulous "swim bladder problems," this condition can also be from indigestion, inner ear problems, or even old age. The only one with a hopeful prognosis is indigestion, and in this case a rest in a hospital tank with some vegetable-based foods given sparingly may bring the fish around in a few days.

Fat as a Blimp!

When fish get fat, or gravid (a female full of eggs, ready to spawn), their bellies may bulge, but if the fish is grossly distended with its scales lifted up away from the body, this is not good. Once labeled "dropsy," this condition is caused by organ failure that permits fluids to build up in the body. Kidney disease, liver disease, septicemia, cancer, and other problems can all produce this symptom.

A veterinarian can take a culture and inject the appropriate antibiotics into the fish to combat a severe kidney infection, but even then there is not a lot of hope. When kidney or liver failure is caused by anything other than bacteria, even this extreme effort will not help.

Fancy goldfish are notorious for suffering swimming disorders.

The best plan here is to prevent problems in the first place with plenty of clean water and a proper diet so that your fish do not contract serious infections.

Pop Eyes

Sometimes a fish will have a fluid buildup behind the eyes, causing the eyes to bulge out and leading to the common designation "pop eye." Some fish have naturally bulgy eyes, and some strains of goldfish have been developed with extremely bulging eyes. This, of course, is not the same thing.

Unfortunately, pop eye is not usually curable, as it usually indicates the end phase of an infection. On rare occasions, and especially if only one eye is involved, it may be the result of injury, pathology, and it will subside on its own as the fish heals, the same way your swollen ankle would.

Preventive Measures

During the height of the cold and flu season, do you ever wish that you and your family could live in a glass bowl, away from all the sniffling, sneezing people? Well, your fish *do* live in an environment that effectively isolates them from other fish that might be sick.

When you buy a new fish, if you just add it to your tank and it is carrying a disease, you wind up instead with a situation analogous to living in a glass bowl along with a bunch of sniffling, sneezing people!

Therefore, when you bring home new fish, they should be quarantined away from your other fish until you are sure that they are not carrying any diseases that could infect your collection. A quarantine tank can also double as a hospital tank if one of your fish gets sick.

A Quarantine Aquarium

The tank need not be large. It is best if it is bare, with no gravel. Hiding places

Exophthalmia is the scientific term for "pop-eye" disease.

can be pieces of plastic pipe or some plastic plants. A small air-driven sponge filter is fine. (If you keep it always running in your main tank, you will have a mature biofilter when you need one for the hospital tank.) A heater and a lid complete the accommodations. A setup like this is easy to clean and does not afford parasites or other pathogens places to hide and reproduce.

Whenever you bring in new fish, or if you have sick fish needing isolation and treatment, you can fill this tank with water from your aquarium and be ready in a few minutes.

Chapter 5

Fish Behavior Problems Solved!

Not all aquarium problems deal with the water or equipment. Sometimes the fish themselves are causing a problem. You might be surprised to learn that fish behavior can be quite complex, and that individual fish can differ greatly from other fish of the same species.

A fish's behavior can change quite rapidly. This can be either a negative or a positive change, and it can be brought about by illness, maturation, breeding readiness, or changes in the environment. (Here "environment" includes tankmates.) Let's start with the most drastic change—from presence to absence.

My Fish Is Missing!

You walk in, take a look in your tank…and your favorite fish is gone! There are many possibilities here, not all bad. Let's consider various scenarios.

A Jumper

It is possible, of course, that your fish has jumped out of the tank. Immediately check the area around the tank (including behind it) for your fish. If you find it on the floor, no matter what it looks like, put it into a jar filled with water from the aquarium. Many dried out, fuzzy, "rug jerky" jumpers have revived when placed back in water.

Use a jar so that if it is dead, you won't have to dig around the tank with your net to get it out, and if it is alive, it will be able to recover without being picked on by its tankmates. Once it is cleaned off, breathing normally, and swimming around, you can put it back in its tank—after you've found and plugged the escape hole.

See the next chapter for a more detailed discussion of how to prevent jumpers.

Endler's livebearers are accomplished jumpers.

A Lost Body

Of course, your fish may still be in the tank, but dead. It may be wedged behind a rock or in a plant. It may be floating up in a corner, behind the heater, or under a filter return. It may also have been sucked up against the filter strainer.

You may, however, never find the body, or at least not much of it. The other fish in the tank, along with snails if you have them, can tear apart and consume a fish carcass rather quickly. This is perfectly natural, but it can be disconcerting the first time you witness it.

Hide and Seek

Often, fortunately, a missing fish is still in the aquarium but hiding. Some fish almost always lurk in a cave, at least when the lights are on, but we're talking here about a fish that used to be out swimming around and suddenly disappears into a cave or crevice somewhere in the tank.

Some fish will burrow into the gravel, completely disappearing from sight. Again, this is natural for certain species, but I have seen fish driven into the gravel by a particularly aggressive tankmate.

It is not necessary to dismantle your aquarium every time a fish goes out of sight. That represents a lot of stress for all the inhabitants of the tank. It is best not to let dead fish decompose unnoticed, but as I

Fish Proof Your Tank

When you set up your aquarium, keep your fish in mind. Do not create places where they can get caught, and minimize hiding spots that are not visible.

mentioned, in many cases the carcass is quickly disposed of.

Remember if you do search for a fish to check the tank from all sides and from the top. (A fish hiding at the surface behind the front top plastic frame is invisible from the front glass.) If you move rocks or other objects, you cannot assume that the fish is not hiding in them, since as you move on to other objects, it may sneak back into one you've already checked. Your search should be mostly visual, with the least possible disturbance to the aquarium.

Once you find the fish, you can begin to judge the reason for its disappearance. Is it cowering, its fins clamped, or is it defending its cavern, poised in the entrance, daring all comers?

If due to the first reason, the fish may be getting picked on, or else it is sick. In either case, you must intervene, and the first thing to do is to get the fish into a quarantine or hospital tank.

Plecos are often seen peering out of their hiding places.

If due to the second reason, the fish has matured and is displaying territoriality. In fact, in some cases, closer inspection will reveal that the fish is guarding a clutch of eggs. Depending on the species, it may be the male, the female, or both that guard the eggs and fry.

Also depending on species, the breeding fish may become a danger to other fish in the tank. If it appears to be ignoring any fish that does not come close to its lair, just keep an eye on things. If, however, it is attacking fish in a large perimeter around its cave, you may have to remove the tankmates to protect them.

Hide and Return

Sometimes a fish defies all attempts to locate it and then suddenly reappears, healthy and happy. Often this is a fish like a loach or a catfish that enjoys trying out every nook and cranny as a potential home. Many times the fish will be so tightly wedged inside an ornament that it does not let go even when the object is removed from the tank for inspection.

Again, unless your tank is experiencing an ammonia spike, there is no need to tear the place apart looking for a missing fish. If it shows up again, great! If not, well, at least you haven't terrorized all your fish.

Calm Down!

You walk in, take a look in your tank…and your fish are going crazy! They're slamming around, smashing into the glass, jumping out of the water. What's going on? (Some fish will act this way when they are first put into a tank, but they soon calm down. We're assuming here that all your fish were well settled into the tank.)

First, take stock. Is it all of the fish, or just some? If it is only a few fish, look to see if another fish is chasing them, trying to drive them out of its territory. This can happen when fish mature and get ready to spawn; they drive away all other fish. In the wild, the other fish just swim out of harm's way, but in an aquarium, they cannot get away, and the territorial fish may kill them. In such cases, you must remove either the aggressor or the victims.

If all the fish in the tank are acting skittish, there is probably something wrong with the conditions in the tank. High concentrations of pollutants, especially nitrites, can cause these symptoms. Test your water. Also check the temperature. When water gets too warm, the fish may

School Zone

Schooling fishes will not behave normally if kept singly or in pairs. You need to keep at least six of their species, preferably more, to observe natural schooling behaviors.

act this way in an effort to get away from the heat.

If everything checks out, do a little detective work around the tank. Did something fall off a bookshelf, maybe hitting the tank? Does the family cat have wet paws? Is there a newly placed motor running that is vibrating the tank?

Whether you find the cause or not, the best treatment is to make a massive water change, but if you know the cause, you can address it to prevent the bad conditions from returning.

Hey! Slow Down!

You walk in, take a look in your tank…and the fish are racing around the tank in fast

Large cichlids, like these Uaru, will often cruise their tanks in pairs.

forward! They aren't bumping into things or acting frantic, but they just won't stop.

The most common cause of this behavior is spawning. Many fish, especially cyprinids (goldfish, barbs, loaches) spawn in groups, with all the males in the tank fervently chasing the females, often through plant thickets. They do not stop for egglaying; the females broadcast the eggs as they swim, the males fertilizing them as they pass. Typically any non-spawning fish follow this crowd, greedily gobbling up the eggs as fast as they are laid, so all the fish in the tank may be involved in the chase.

This is perfectly natural, and all will soon return to normal, when the fish have finished spawning and join their tankmates in searching out any remaining eggs for a snack. Depending on what fish you have in the tank, and what sort of aquascaping you have, an occasional fry or two might survive, though it is not common in a community setting. If you would like to try to breed your fish and produce a batch of juveniles, you will need to set up a separate tank and follow certain procedures, which will vary depending on what species of fish you want to spawn.

Break It Up, Guys!

You walk in, take a look in your tank…and the fish are fighting! The extent of the battling varies depending on the species involved. Male bettas and many cichlids may tear pieces out of each other and even fight to the death; male swordtails usually only inflict minor injuries; and most tetras are all bluff and bluster.

Danio species are fast movers in aquariums!

Oscars may argue with each other over territory.

Fish in the wild do not go around beating each other up. Yes, there are fish that will attack other fish and eat them, but that is not aggression—it's predation. Real aggression between two fish will usually only last as long as the weaker fish persists. When it is ready to give up, the loser will swim rapidly away, and the victor will stay put and gloat.

In an aquarium, however, there is nowhere for the loser to retreat. Chances are that the victor will still be able to see it. This signifies to the victor that the other fish has not given up—since it's still in the victor's territory—and it continues the assault.

Realizing this makes it much easier to understand your fish's behavior. After all, it doesn't make sense for spawning pairs or competing territory holders to fight to the death. Fighting among fishes most often serves the purpose of establishing the fitness and strength of the combatants. The winners get along quite well, but the losers survive to gain strength and

fight again another day. In an aquarium we must intervene to protect the weaker fish.

If you do have cichlids, and just one pair is fighting, and both fish seem to be holding their ground, it could be normal mating behavior. What looks like combat is actually a type of fitness test. By jaw wrestling and slapping at each other, head to tail and tail to head, each fish can judge how strong and healthy the other fish is. You can leave them together as long as it doesn't appear that one fish is injuring the other, and they both seem interested in the contest. As soon as one of them begins trying to hide from the other, you must intervene, or you will soon have a dead body to remove from the tank.

If each member of the pair finds the other fit, they will move on to the next stages of spawning behavior—which might take the shape of beating up all the other fish in the tank.

Spawning Behavior

Various aggressive behaviors are associated with breeding in many species. Males (and sometimes females) fight over territories. Pairs defend a territory against all intruders. One or both parents defend the eggs or the fry. This defense can range from simply keeping potential predators out of reach of the brood to massacring all the other fish in the tank. Cichlids and catfish are most often the types involved in this kind of behavior.

Often these fish live quite peaceably in a community before they pair up and spawn, at which point the tank becomes a war zone. The only solution in such a case is to remove either the breeding pair or their tankmates.

Territoriality

Some species of fish establish a territory and hold it against all comers, completely outside of any breeding behavior. Again this is something that manifests during maturation, so the aquarist is often dismayed that a peaceful fish has become so belligerent. Red tail sharks definitely fall into this category. They are fairly peaceful when young, but as they mature, they develop more and more of a temper. Depending on the size of your tank, it may soon be too small for anyone other than the red tail shark.

The best solution is prevention. The advice is repeated so often because it is so important: Read about any species of

Many cichlids, like this firemouth, are very protective of their fry

fish before purchasing it, to save yourself an enormous amount of hassle.

Nasties

There are some species of fish, typically large ones, that simply want to be the only fish in the tank. They seem to be unable to stand the sight of any other fish and will attack it until it is dead. This is unrelated to breeding behavior—in fact, the fish may eliminate proffered mates as well.

Although biologists will explain this as general territoriality, which in the confines of an aquarium becomes murderous, many aquarists insist that these fish are downright grumpy. Whichever explanation you prefer, fish like this need to be kept as single specimens. On the positive side, they often make delightful pets, recognizing their owner and genuinely interacting through the glass.

Predation

I said above that predation isn't aggression, and normally it isn't. However, the same wild-captive difference as in aggression can occur with predation. In nature, most attempts by a predator to catch its prey fail, and the prey escapes. In an aquarium, the predator gets as many tries as it wants, and the prey cannot escape.

Many cichlids will try and bounce their tankmates from their hiding spots.

In nature, if a predator tries to capture an animal that is really too big or too fast or too strong to take down, the prey escapes. In an aquarium, the predator gets to attack again and again, sometimes literally tearing the prey to pieces, and the prey cannot escape.

Pike cichlids tend to be very aggressive; keep a close watch on them!

African cichlids can really batter their tankmates.

It is not only the large predators that can appear murderous in captive conditions. Some small predatory fish can be just as relentless and merciless in their pursuit. In addition, certain stimuli elicit predatory behavior very strongly, and normally peaceful fish can become ferocious. Here's an example:

Neon tetras are very beautiful, very small, very popular fish. They also appear to taste really, really good. At least the way other fish go after them would indicate so. I once added a batch of neons to a community tank in which the largest fish were tiger barbs. I followed my own advice and made sure that the neons were easily too large for any of their tankmates to swallow.

Unfortunately, as soon as the neons were in the water, every other fish in the tank went into a shark impression. Fish were swimming crazily around the tank, each with a neon's head or tail shoved into its mouth. None of the fish were able to swallow the neons, as I had planned, but within seconds they were all dead nonetheless.

Mismatched Tankmates

Certain species simply don't get along with each other, and sometimes individual fish do not get along. Slow feeders like discus cannot get their fair share if kept with greedy feeders like clown loaches. A pleco and a cichlid might each claim the same cave and fight constantly. Nippy fish like tiger barbs cannot resist a betta's or an angelfish's long flowing fins.

Speaking of tiger barbs, they provide an example of how knowing a species' habits and behaviors is important. Tiger barbs are schooling fish, and the dynamic relationships within the school are part of the normal behavior for these fish. The members spend a good portion of every day chasing each other all over the place. Robbed of these interactions, these playful barbs look elsewhere for an outlet for their nervous energy. Very often two or three tiger barbs in a tank will be very nippy, annoying other fish and biting long fins. Bring that number up to eight or more, and very often the obnoxious behavior stops. The barbs spend so much time cavorting and playing tag that they leave their tankmates alone.

African Cichlid Paradox

When dealing with the cichlids known as "mbuna," aquarists have to deal with an extreme level of aggression. These fish live in great numbers on rocky reefs in Lake Malawi, where territory is in short supply, and competition for everything, from food to mates, is very fierce. As an adaptation, these fish have very small territories, very short tempers, and very short attention spans. They will brutally attack any fish that comes near, unless it's a female ready to spawn, but once the interloper moves a short distance away, it cuts off the chase

Klingon Rituals?

The displays and wrestling many fish perform as part of the mating ritual may seem maladaptive in an aquarium, but in the wild they work quite well. Remember that the signal to call off an aggressive attack for most fish is the disappearance of the subordinate animal. If the pursued fish cannot get out of sight of its attacker, it will be perceived as wishing to continue the contest.

before someone else takes over his territory while his back is turned.

In the confines of an aquarium their extreme aggression can result in extreme bloodshed. A common method of handling this fish is first to fill the tank with lots of rock piles, providing both plenty of visual cues for territories and plenty of hiding holes where fish can escape out of sight of each other. Then the fish are stocked at a very high level; the sheer number of fish means that no particular one or few will get picked on all the time.

It is sometimes difficult to achieve the proper balance. Too few cichlids, and you'll have one or two dominant ones beating on all the others. Too many, and you'll overtax the tank and the biofilter. You must make sure that no one male becomes dominant. If he does, he will begin eliminating all other male fish (not just the same species), and many of the females as well.

Eliminating Territories

A variant of this technique is often used in wholesale and retail fish businesses. Fish are stocked at high density in bare tanks. The lack of hiding places is not a big problem because there are so many fish to diffuse any aggression; a pursued fish can get lost in the crowd. The lack of visual cues makes it impossible for dominant fish to establish boundary lines for territories, so territoriality is kept to a minimum. It's not the best setup, but it works as a temporary solution.

Aggression Toward Human Beings

What about fish attacking their human caretakers? Is that a concern? Well, first of all, I would hope that you would not be keeping fish which can seriously injure or kill you. Yes, there are fish in those categories! Highly venomous and electricity-generating species (i.e., electric eels, electric catfish, and large sorubim catfish) have no place in the

All cichlids are highly defensive of their young-no matter the size of the intruder!

casual aquarist's aquarium, and I would hope no reputable dealer will sell them to you.

There are, however, non-lethal species that can still injure you or cause you pain. Fortunately, in almost all cases these are fishes that are not going to attack you aggressively; they may, however, inflict injury if mishandled or threatened. Many fish have sharp spines which they use for defense against predators. Catfish and loaches especially have some very impressive blades, some of which are normally retracted and only extended when the animal is scared. Sometimes there are venom glands at the base of these spines.

You Can't Punish Fish

Children often want to control aggressive behavior in their fish. Explain that you cannot punish fish, nor teach them not to fight.

It is very common for such fish to become horribly entangled in the mesh of a fish net. In an effort to release the poor writhing fish, the aquarist can easily be poked. If the fish is venomous, toxin can be injected into a hand or arm. While not life threatening, such envenomation can be extremely painful, and the wound may take a long time to heal.

Another source of human injury is being spiked while servicing the aquarium. If you are careless when you have your hand in the tank for regular cleaning, planting, or aquascaping activities, you can brush up against a spined fish and get struck by it.

It is your responsibility to know your fish. Read about any species before purchasing it, and if a fish *can* injure you, handle it extremely carefully and keep a close eye on it during tank maintenance.

There are some fish that will attack you on purpose. Almost any cichlid that cares for its fry will attack a hand that enters the water near its brood. The ferocity of the attack does not depend on the size of the fish, but the outcome does. A 3-inch (7.5-cm) cichlid's repeated bites feel like gentle pinches, while a 12 in. (30 cm) fish might draw blood.

What's That Noise?

Aquarists are sometimes spooked by noises coming from their aquarium. Various croaks and clicks can sometimes be heard across the room. Some fish make noises in many situations, including territorial disputes. In almost all cases, these are not fish vocalizations; fish make noises when they manipulate bones against each other, producing snapping or grinding sounds.

The most common species to be heard like this are various catfish and some loaches. When quarreling over some live blackworms, clown loaches can make a clicking sound that is astonishingly loud.

Even expected fish sounds like splashing at the surface can be more extreme than you'd think. Many fish actually take to the air (which is one reason why you need a good cover on the tank), and even a very small fish can make quite a splash this way. Large fish can actually get you wet; I have some large cichlids that routinely send water flying a couple of feet from their tank— and that's just for sport. At feeding time, the water appears as if it's boiling.

71

Fish Behavior Problems Solved!

Chapter 6

Fish Fatality Problems Solved!

The unexpected death of a fish is obviously a cause for concern. We're talking here about fish that are not showing symptoms of disease, as when the first indication that anything is wrong is death.

Ugh! Rug Jerky!

We already discussed this problem in Chapter 5 from the point of view of solving the problem of a missing fish. In this chapter, however, we are looking at ways of preventing tragedies, so other than trying to resuscitate the jumper, what can be done?

If your aquarium has a full hood or canopy, you may wonder how the fish got out. The smallest openings can often permit a fish to escape. Spaces for filters or heaters can be sufficiently large. If you have any openings in the tank cover that are the same size as your fish or larger, cover them with pieces of glass, plastic, or even cardboard.

Now, some fish don't jump out so much as slither out. These fish go up the side of the tank and start nosing around. If they find a hole large enough, they squirm through it. No, they're not suicidal. Many fish investigate the environment by going up and over obstacles. They have no way of knowing that the tank wall is anything other than something to swim up and over.

Bottom dwellers like spiny eels, catfish, and loaches are especially likely to escape this way because they are used to following the contours of the bottom. Species that spend their lives

Eels are likely to escape from your tank because they follow environmental contours, which in an aquarium includes up and over the glass!

up in the water are not as likely to overshoot the top of the glass.

In the wild, it is a rare fish that gets stranded on land. Even if a fish pulls itself onto the shore, all it has to do is flip when it finds itself out of the water, and it will plop back into the water. Unfortunately, the same behavior in your living room will only move it farther away from the tank, not back in.

Another type of fish that is likely to escape through a hole in the cover are surface dwellers like hatchetfish. Such fish are usually easy to spook, and they often avoid predators, real or imagined, by leaping out of the water. Obviously, in the wild they normally just fall back in, but if their leap puts them out of a tank, they will most likely fall onto the floor, not back through the same hole.

Sometimes it is hard to believe that a fish was able to find a hole and squeeze through it, but such thinking is too purposeful. If a fish often jumps out of the water, given enough time, it will eventually jump out directly under a hole in the cover. In fact, a common lament is from an aquarist who had maintained an aquarium for a long time, and then "suddenly" a fish jumped out.

While small fish can find gaps to jump out through them, large fish can sometimes make their own escape openings. Fish have been known to jump hard enough to crack glass aquarium tops, or to leap so powerfully that they lift the top up and continue on out of the tank before the top crashes back down onto the aquarium. Make sure the top is strong enough

Only Dead Fish Don't Jump

Any fish can jump out of your tank. If you do not have a good cover on your aquarium, you will eventually lose fish, even if you are lucky for a long time. Count on it.

to withstand an impact, and weight it down or lock it in place to keep it from shifting.

A layer of floating plants is an excellent deterrent to jumping. Not only does it present what appears to be a solid surface, it gives fish a sense of security. Since fish are often preyed on from above, they are less flighty when they are not under an open surface.

Hatchetfishes will leap at the first sign of danger.

My New Fish Died!

When your fish dies the first day you have it, the cause is almost certainly stress. It may have had something wrong with it, and the stress of moving it to your tank (the stress of netting, transporting, acclimation, and a new environment) proved to be the last straw.

It is also possible, however, that your acclimation—or lack thereof—is to blame. There are many ideas about acclimating new arrivals, some much better than others. In fact, the most common method is one of the worst ways of doing this important task: floating the bag in your tank for 20 minutes and then releasing the fish.

The argument here is that this equalizes the temperature, getting the water in the bag to the same temperature as the aquarium water. This is an important thing, but floating the bag is not the way to do it. For one thing, it puts the bag up near the light, which can easily heat the water in the bag much higher than the water in the tank—the exact opposite of what you desire.

More important, it focuses only on temperature. While you certainly don't want to shock your fish by plunging them into much cooler or warmer water than they are in, there are many other ways in which you can shock your fish which are not eliminated by floating the bag.

Remember that a fish's gills are

Did My Filter Kill My Fish?

Many people think their filter has killed a fish when they find a corpse plastered against the intake siphon, but this is misplaced blame. The suction of even the most powerful filters is not sufficient to hold a fish of any size against its will. Very small fry can be sucked up or against a filter tube, but that is all. When a fish dies, it becomes an inanimate object, and like any other debris floating around in the water, it can be drawn by the filter's suction.

extremely sensitive organs, in which the fish's bloodstream is only a few cells away from the water in which the fish swims. The chemistry of water includes a variety of parameters, just some of which are salinity, pH, hardness, and alkalinity. Most aquarium fish are extremely adaptable to various water chemistries; that is, they can live in a wide range of values. They cannot, however, tolerate extremely rapid changes in chemistries of any type. If the chemistry of the water in your aquarium is drastically different from

Congo tetras are hardy fish after they have been in the tank for a while.

that of the water in which the fish arrives, the chemical shock can kill the fish outright, or weaken it so badly that it succumbs a little later.

Acclimating your fish means matching the chemistry of the water in which they're swimming to the chemistry of the water in the tank into which they will be placed. Fortunately you do not have to perform any tests, take any measurements, or adjust the water with various chemical compounds. All you need is patience and a piece of airline tubing.

Proper Acclimation

The proper acclimation of new fish purchases not only keeps them from receiving severe shocks, it also prevents introducing any disease organisms or unwanted chemicals that are in the water within the bag into your system. Here are the simple steps:

- Gently empty the bag(s) into a container that can hold several times the volume of the original water in the bag.

- Take a length of airline tubing, and tie a loose knot in it.

- Put one end of the tubing into the aquarium, and suck on the other to start a siphon.

- As soon as the water begins to flow, tighten the knot until the water is merely dripping slowly from the tubing into the container. You want just a drop or two per second.

- When the original volume of water in the container has doubled or tripled, stop the drip, and net the fish out of the container and release them into the tank.

This method equalizes all water conditions, including temperature, between the aquarium and the water the new fish are swimming in. It takes a while, but it's time and effort very well spent.

Quarantine & Introduction

Most aquarists do not quarantine new fish. They should, but they don't bother. Some aquarists are quarantine fanatics; these are invariably those who have had a major wipeout. What usually happens is that a large collection of expensive fish is decimated by a disease brought in by an inexpensive fish added thoughtlessly to the tank.

In Chapter 4 we talked about the importance of quarantine, both for protecting your collection and for resting your new acquisitions. Quarantine can make the difference between life and death for a new fish. Even if it is properly acclimated, a new fish can be so stressed by its being placed into your aquarium that it will be floating belly-up the next morning.

At the end of a few weeks quarantine, you know that your new fish are healthy. They have adapted to your water and food. They have recovered from the stress of transport and sale. They still have a major disadvantage in terms of joining the other fish in your aquarium—they are newcomers.

The fish in an established aquarium have worked out a social organization. They all know who the dominant fish are, and where everyone's territorial boundaries are. When new fish are and gives the newcomers a more even chance. It is also a good idea to introduce the fish at night, after the lights are turned off. This enables them to begin to orient themselves to the tank before they have to deal with their tankmates.

Half My Fish Died!

The sudden death of many fish in your tank is cause for immediate concern, of course. This is an indication that something is seriously wrong. Though this can be due to disease, usually some symptoms will show up before that kind of death toll appreciates.

For environmental conditions to become lethal at this level requires a serious breakdown in aquarium maintenance. A malfunctioning heater might be the cause, but usually you will notice this before a massive die-off.

We are assuming here that this is not a recently set-up tank. It is not at all uncommon for most or all of the fish to die if they are simply put into an uncycled tank. We covered cycling in Chapter 1, of course. Even in a cycled tank, however, an ammonia kill is possible.

Proper acclimation of all fishes is a must! Make sure that any rocks used in decorating your tank are non-reactive (inert).

added, they are going to have to fight everybody else to determine their place in the hierarchy and to get their own territories…or not.

If you rearrange the decor in the tank before adding the new fish, this breaks up the established territories

Sudden Ammonia Spike

If the biofilter in your aquarium is compromised, you can get ammonia and nitrite accumulations. This can happen due to medications or other chemicals killing off some of the bacteria, or it can be caused by major temperature changes. It can even be caused by cleaning your filter too well, removing a portion of your biofilter. Washing the biomedium in tap water that has chlorine or chloramine in it can kill off the bacterial colonies; instead, always use aquarium water to rinse biomedia.

Another cause of ammonia or nitrite spikes is from a sudden increase in the bioload, which overwhelms the biofilter and exceeds its capacity to handle the wastes. This can be caused by a dead fish, a die-off of plants or algae, or the addition of several large fish. An ammonia spike can also be caused by a water change if the water is not properly conditioned.

Water Sanitizers

Municipal water systems use a variety of chemical sanitizers to kill bacteria in the drinking water. Most vary the chemicals used and the amounts added to the water supply. The two most common are chlorine and chloramine. Chlorine is easily neutralized with a solution of sodium thiosulfate. If, however, you use thiosulfate to condition water that contains

Some fish are particularly sensitive to ammonia spikes.

chloramine, the chlorine part of the molecule is neutralized, but ammonia is released. Instead of clean water, you'd be adding ammonia solution to your aquarium!

What you need to use is a product specifically designed to neutralize chloramine. You should use this to condition your tap water unless you are positive your water company never uses anything other than chlorine.

Poisoning

Aquarium fish are occasionally poisoned in other following ways:

- The use of insecticides near or around an aquarium can result in the rapid death of all the fish. If insecticides must be used, the aquarium must be hermetically sealed under plastic. Don't forget to turn off the air pump, or it will deliver the poison directly to the tank. Even with these precautions, fumes may get in.

- Another source of poison fumes that can harm or kill your fish is interior painting. When the room in which the aquarium is located is painted, the tank should be covered tightly in plastic, with the air pump off.

- Smoke is toxic to fish. If people smoke in your home, toxins can accumulate in the water sufficient to harm your fish. Frequent water changes will help keep them diluted.

- Likewise, a kitchen isn't the best place for an aquarium. Aerosol cooking oils, cooking smoke, and kitchen cleansers are all potential dangers.

- Chemical residues on your skin can dissolve in the aquarium and kill your fish. Washing your hands may not be enough to remove these. If you handle harsh chemicals, wear protective gloves when you service your tank.

- Never use anything other than water to clean the outside glass of an aquarium. Even if you are careful not

SMALL FRY

Dealing with Death

The death of pet fish can be part of a child's learning about life and its dangers. Children can become very attached to their fish on an individual basis. Don't underestimate a child's mourning, but use the experience to express positive ideas such as supporting each other and remembering the pet for good.

to spray any glass cleaner into the tank, minute drops and fumes can easily enter the water, poisoning the fish.

How Old Do Fish Get?

Obviously, fish can die of old age. The majority of common aquarium species will live for several years, but many cichlids and catfish can live for a couple of decades. Generally speaking, larger fish tend to live longer, while the smallest species have the shortest lives. There also seems to be considerable individual variation, even more than among cats, dogs, horses, or humans.

Chapter 7

Equipment Problems Solved!

Okay, we've discussed problems with your cycling, your water, your tank, your fish's health, and your fish's behavior. That leaves just the ancillary equipment attached to your aquarium. Much of this equipment can be considered the life support system for your fish, and problems with it can be very serious.

My Pump Won't Pump!

Most aquarium systems rely on an air pump, a water pump, or both. These are used both for filtration and for water movement and aeration. When they cease to function, conditions in the aquarium can deteriorate rapidly. It is a good idea to have a spare on hand, but let's look at the various problems that may cause a pump to fail.

Ah! Vibration!

Although piston air pumps were once popular, they have been replaced by modern vibrator pumps. As you can tell from their name, these pumps have a vibrating motor that is the mechanism that pumps the air.

Many of the problems with vibration noises are caused by imbalance. Usually this is from the pump being on a non-level surface, or being in touch with a rigid or unstable object. In the first case, the pump itself vibrates erratically, producing the noise; and in the second, the object touching the pump resonates with the pump's vibration, producing noise. Obviously, both situations are corrected by placing the pump on a solid, level surface. The use of a foam or other non-rigid pad under the pump will prevent its vibration from being transferred to the table or shelf on which it sits.

The other cause of vibration noise is from the pump producing more air than the system to which it is connected can handle. This causes back pressure, which, besides being noisy, reduces the life of the pump. There are two ways to handle this, the first being to increase the outlets. If you have nowhere else to use the air, you can open a valve at the end of the line, bleeding off enough of the surplus to quiet the pump. If your pump has an adjustable air output, you can also turn it down until the noise stops.

Airstones provide much-needed oxygen to your fishes-not by way of the bubbles but rather by way of the surface movement the bubbles produce.

Airstones Are Not Forever

Even if you have an air filter in your supply line, an airstone will eventually become clogged with minute particles of dirt that get wedged in the pores, decreasing the output of bubbles—and increasing the strain on your air pump. Fortunately, airstones are cheap. When they slow down, toss them out and replace with new ones.

No Air!

You may find that your air pump is still vibrating away, but there is very little air coming out. First confirm that the pump is the problem by removing the airline and checking to see if air is pumping out from the unit itself. If it is, the problem is farther down the line.

In hard water, a buildup of scale (lime) can completely block the end of an airline that is underwater. The solution for that is to snip off the blockage and reattach the line at the clean cut.

If the problem is diminished output, it is likely that the pump's diaphragm(s) need replacing. The rubber diaphragms can wear out or tear. In either case, the bellows-like effect is impeded. You can purchase repair kits for most models that will quickly and easily restore the pump to its original output, and it is a wise move to have a kit in reserve.

If an airpump with two outlets has not been in use long enough to justify worn out diaphragms, you may have an imbalance between the outlets, which causes the diaphragms to wear prematurely. The proper way to hook these pumps up is to attach a short piece of tubing to each outlet, then attach both of them to a tee (a small plastic or brass fitting that allows one airline to be split into two). Then attach the tubing that feeds your various devices to the third leg of the tee. In such a setup, there is an even backpressure on each diaphragm, and they wear evenly.

Water Pump Problems

Water pumps, sometimes also known as powerheads, are not usually part of a first aquarium setup, but you may very well be using one or more of them in your tank. These submersible water pumps are quite reliable, but problems can develop.

Different Circuits

Plug your aquarium's equipment into plugs serviced by different circuit breakers, if possible. That way, if one circuit trips, you won't lose all the life support.

Loud sucking or gurgling noises are typical when the powerhead's intake is at the surface. Restoring the water level should fix the problem quickly. Occasionally air becomes trapped inside the powerhead. Simply tip the pump from side to side while completely underwater, and the air will bubble out.

My Filter Won't Work!

Each filter design creates its own opportunities for problems, but these all fall into general categories.

Failure to Start

The most common cause of starting problems is the loss of a prime. Almost all hang-on filters operate by suctioning water up from the tank and pumping it through the filter; it then returns to the tank by gravity. The standard outside filter needs to be primed—filled with water—in order for the pump to be able to pull water up from the tank.

Having the water too low on either side of the siphon will cause the prime to break, and the pump will labor in vain to pull water

into the filter from the aquarium. Thus, if the water level falls too low in the tank, or if there is insufficient water in the filter compartments, the prime will be lost.

Keep in mind that the pump can *maintain* a prime under conditions in which it cannot *establish* a prime. That is, as long as water does not stop flowing, the filter will continue operating even with reduced water

Canister filters are very powerful and efficient.

Don't Inhale!

Sucking on the far end of a siphon tube is a colorful way of starting water flowing out of your aquarium, but it's not necessary. If you are using a short hose, simply put the whole thing into the tank and maneuver it until all the air is out. Then plug one end with your thumb and put it into the bucket while leaving the other end in the tank, under the water's surface. Now simply release your thumb, and the siphon starts. With a longer hose, put the gravel tube underwater, then lift it up so the water it contains drains into the hose. A couple of tries will usually start the siphon successfully.

levels in the aquarium. If the water flow is broken however, as by a power loss, the pump may not be able to restart when power is restored. Sometimes replacing the water in the filter itself is sufficient, but with really low water levels, you'll need to refill the aquarium, too. Of course, it's never a good idea to let the water level drop that much in the first place.

Clogged Media

For maximum efficiency, filters are designed not to allow channeling, which is when the water finds a path of least resistance through the medium, bypassing it and exiting the unit largely unfiltered. This means, however, that if the medium becomes so saturated with dirt that the water flow through the medium is impaired, the water flow through the filter will decrease.

Some filter designs have a back channel through which the water is diverted in such a case, alerting the aquarist to the problem, and others have meters built in that indicate when the flow is inadequate. With any filter, however, you can notice when the return flow has decreased. The solution, of course, is to clean or replace the filter media, restoring unimpeded flow and normal output.

It is important to operate the filter the way in which the manufacturer describes in order to avoid a more serious case of clogged media. For example, mechanical filtration properly takes place first, trapping suspended debris before the water arrives at the biofiltration medium. Since micropores are the heart of a biofilter, if you do not have the proper mechanical filter medium in place ahead of the biomedium, the latter will quickly get clogged with dirt.

Aside from a rapid decline in the water flow through the filter, this may result in the destruction of the

biomedium. Foam, ceramic, and carbon media can be very difficult to clean when they are plugged with particles of debris, and they may need to be replaced. This means, of course, that you may have to recycle the tank, since you are removing the biofilter.

Plugged Holes

Many filters, especially those with biowheels or spraybar returns, rely on water spraying from a series of holes along a tube. The design places these holes after the filtration media, so they cannot usually be plugged by dirt. They can, however, get clogged by algae or with calcium deposits left behind when hard water evaporates.

The solution is usually as easy as taking a toothpick and clearing the holes so that they all permit normal water flow. In cases in which the white crust is particularly thick and hard, soaking the tube in a small dish of vinegar for a half hour or so will loosen the scale so you can clean it off.

Impeller Problems

The impeller is the heart of a power filter. It normally sits at the base of the siphon uptake tube that conducts water out of the tank; it sucks water up from the tank and pushes it out into the media. If it is not operating properly, water will not flow properly through the filter.

The instructions that came with your filter will describe how to remove and clean the impeller. A very common problem that slows down an impeller is fibrous material getting wrapped around it. Usually this is hair algae or some other plant material. In the same way that tall weeds can get wrapped around a mower blade or tiller tines, this material is wound around the impeller. You may need to use a small pointed tool to remove it if it is wrapped too tightly to pull off.

You may be surprised at what you find when you open up a filter with impeller problems. If you do not have an adequate strainer on the uptake tube, a dead fish, chunk of plant, or some foreign object like a rubber band may have gotten sucked into the filter and jammed around the impeller. Live fish have been known to swim up the tube and meet their demise in the whirling impeller.

The impeller is the only moving part in many filters, and after whirring away 24-7, it can become worn or broken over time. In this case replacing it with a new one can greatly rejuvenate the filter.

Almost all filter impellers are magnetic driven; a magnet attached to the impeller spins in a well in the plastic filter body, a socket surrounded by the magnetic drive motor. This magnet and the hole into which it fits may get clogged with dirt, which will also impede the operation of the impeller.

Why Is the Filter So Noisy?

Most modern aquarium filters are virtually noiseless in operation. Usually the trickle of water is louder than any humming or buzz from the filter motor. If a filter loses its prime, it may make a

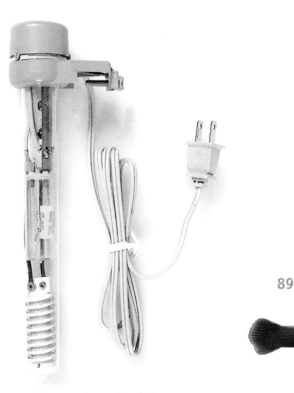

Hang-on-the-tank style heaters are common in smaller aquariums.

chugging or gurgling sound, which is good, since it alerts you to reprime it.

A rattling sound usually indicates an impeller problem, with the rattle being caused by the magnet spinning irregularly, hitting the sides of the well in which it sits. Checking and cleaning or replacing the impeller will often solve this.

Sometimes people object to the sound of the water returning to the aquarium. Often just raising the water level in the aquarium slightly so the water will not fall so far will solve the problem. If not, you can adjust the water flow to eliminate the noise; almost all filters have a means of regulating the volume of the flow, the angle of the flow, or both.

My Heater's Stuck!

A heater is crucial to most aquarium setups, so crucial that many aquarists throw out the heaters and replace them with a new one(s) each a year. Typically these are people who have had a disaster due to a broken heater. Heaters can certainly operate for many years, but if they malfunction, they can cook your fish.

Broken Glass

Many heaters have their components sealed in a glass tube. A hard blow can break the glass, shorting out the heater. Aquarists very commonly forget to unplug the heater when doing a water change. The high-and-dry heater becomes very hot, and when the tank is refilled, the cool water cracks the glass. This usually does not present a problem for the fish, but if you stick your hand into the tank, you can get quite a shock, since you provide a ground for the current.

Heaters with unbreakable stainless steel or titanium tubes are becoming more popular, and some models have sensors that turn off the heating element when the heater is removed from the water. Ask your favorite pet retailer to show you the different models that are available.

Thermostat Problems

When a heater's indicator light stays on but it does not produce heat, obviously the device is broken and needs to be replaced, as it does when it sticks in the on position and just keeps pumping out heat no matter how low you adjust the setting. It is always a good idea to have a spare heater on hand for such situations.

Another approach is to divide the total wattage between two or more heaters; if you need 150 watts to heat the tank, use two 75-watt heaters, for example. This protects against both extremes. If the heater sticks on, the functioning unit will stay off if the water overheats, making the rise in temperature slower. In the event that one heater fails completely, the other one will keep the temperature from becoming dangerously low.

Thermometers are important tools that allow you to gauge how your heater is working.

Beating the Weather

If your aquarium becomes too hot due to summer weather, replace the solid top with a screen one and position a fan to blow over the water. This increases evaporation, which can lower the water temperature.

Hey, I Got a Shock!

Unlike water and oil, water and electricity do mix—but with potentially lethal consequences! If you receive a shock when you touch a piece of equipment or stick your hand into the water, this is a very serious matter, and you should unplug all electrical devices until you have discovered and remedied the problem. Much better still is to prevent such problems in the first place by using the correct setup. Whenever water and electricity are known to be in proximity (kitchens, bathrooms, swimming pools, etc.) special protection is required by law. You should feel a similar urgency about protecting your aquarium installation.

We've already mentioned the possibility of an aquarium becoming electrically charged by a broken heater, making touching the water much like sticking your finger into an electrical outlet. Many other hazards also exist, both from equipment failure and from human intervention, such as dropping the aquarium light into the water. Let's look at several important things you can do to protect yourself, your family, and your aquarium.

GF(C)I Devices

Anything electric connected to your aquarium must be plugged into a GF(C)I device. That stands for Ground Fault (Circuit) Interrupting, and it can mean the difference between life and death. Regular circuit breakers only monitor the total flow of electricity; if it exceeds the specified amperage, the breaker trips, cutting off the electricity. A GFI breaker also monitors the difference between the hot and ground sides of the circuit. If the flow through the hot side is greater than the return flow to ground (meaning there is a ground fault, a flow of electricity from the power supply to something other than the proper return to ground), it trips.

Thus, in the event that an electrical device becomes charged, the interrupter will trip the circuit as soon as a ground is completed. So, if a broken heater charges your aquarium water with 120 volts, when you stick in your finger, giving all that electricity a way out to ground through the soles of your feet, a GF(C)I device will trip, and you'll stay standing.

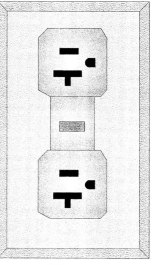

A GFI breaker monitors the difference between current in the hot and neutral sides of a circuit.

There are different ways to get GF(C)I protection:

- A GF(C)I circuit breaker installed for each circuit into which your aquarium devices will be plugged. The circuit breaker affords protection for all outlets on its circuit throughout the house.

- A GF(C)I outlet installed in every box into which your aquarium devices will be plugged. An electrician can replace any duplex outlet with a GF(C)I duplex. This will protect anything plugged into its two outlets.

- A GF(C)I power strip into which all your aquarium devices will be plugged. Anything plugged into the strip is protected. Note that regular power strips or surge protectors are not ground fault protected. You must use one that is specifically rated as GF(C)I.

Air Pump Positioning

When an air pump is placed below the water level of the aquarium, in the event of a power failure, water will siphon back up the airline and drain into the pump. When the power comes back on, this can cause a shock hazard. There are two ways of preventing this: use a check valve, or place the air pump on a shelf higher than the water level. A check valve allows movement in one direction but not the other; thus, air can leave the pump and enter the tank, but water cannot siphon back down the tubing from the tank.

Drip Loops

There are many ways in which water that should be in the aquarium can find its way out of the tank. One that may not be noticed is the condensing of

SMALL FRY

Kid Watch: Hands Off!

Small children must be made to understand from the start that they cannot touch the aquarium's equipment. Cuts, burns, and electric shocks are among the dangers to your child, and your fish could easily be killed by unauthorized manipulation of the equipment.

Cabinet stands allow the hobbyist to conceal the aquarium's equipment.

The wire can be secured with clamps, special staples, or heavy tape.

Secure Equipment

All equipment must be securely attached to the aquarium. Do not use makeshift installations. Specifically:

• Never place an aquarium on or above an electrical appliance like a stereo or a television. Even routine maintenance could send water into the appliance.

fine water spray on some surface above the water level. This water can then drip down wires that are hanging from lighting or other equipment. As it follows the wire, it can find its way into the outlet into which the wire is plugged. A simple drip loop prevents this from happening.

Arrange the cords so that they make a U-shaped loop before they are plugged into the wall outlet. This places the lowest point below the outlet, and any water sliding down the cord will drip off at the lowest point, preventing it from reaching the outlet.

• Always unplug a piece of aquarium equipment before moving it—you might slip and drop it into the water.

• Use only appropriate covers and light fixtures that sit securely and completely on the top frame of the aquarium without wobbling.

• If using a hang-on heater, make sure the clamp is screwed tightly to the tank frame so the heater cannot fall into the tank.

• Make certain that water pumps (pumps, powerheads, power filters) are not allowed to run dry; they can burn out their seals and perhaps start a fire.

Chapter 8

Plant Problems Solved!

Although most problems beginning aquarists face involve either the equipment or the fish, sometimes they have trouble with their live plants. Whether you just want a few plants in your aquarium or you are trying for an aquatic garden with primary emphasis on the plants, not the fish, you need to understand what plants need to thrive.

You certainly have heard that plants "make their own food," but you've also probably seen various products labeled "plant food." So, what gives? Well, all living things need to take in nutrients from their environment. Animals must eat other living things—plants, animals, or both—to provide both the building blocks for their maintenance and growth and the energy they need. For energy animals need fats and carbohydrates, for raw materials they need proteins, and they need some basic nutrients like calcium, phosphorus, and trace elements.

Plants, however, are able to use the energy of the sun, and they store excess energy chemically in carbohydrates like starch and sugar. They also can use nitrogen compounds like ammonia and nitrate directly to make proteins for growth and maintenance. Thus, plants need to take in from the environment, as nutrients, only the most basic building blocks: nitrogen compounds, carbon dioxide, water, phosphorus, potassium, etc. Most aquarium water has plenty of phosphorus and nitrogen compounds from fish food and fish wastes, so they are rarely a cause of problems with aquatic plants. Light and carbon dioxide, however, are often in short supply. Keep this information in mind as we look at some common plant problems and how they can be solved.

A beautifully aquascaped tank takes time and patience to create.

My Plants Are Dying!

Sometimes live plants seem to start failing as soon as they are put into an aquarium, turning brown, dropping leaves, or just apparently melting away into a decaying mess. The most common reason for this is that some plants sold for aquariums are actually terrestrial plants, bog plants that cannot grow fully submerged; some examples are crinkle plant, mondo grass, purple waffle plant, green hedge, and underwater palms. Some aquarists are successful with a particular species, such as the Brazilian sword or peace lily, but even though this plant sometimes remains alive under water, its growth is fully spectacular when kept with just its roots in water.

You should make sure that the plants you buy for your aquarium are true aquatic species. Your dealer should be able to tell you, or you can check reference books or online sources.

A similar but less drastic die-off takes place when aquatic plants that are grown emersed (out of water instead of immersed in water) are placed into an aquarium. In this case the plant is a true aquatic, but it is grown with only its roots in water. Such plants are typically free of diseases and snails, and they are much stronger and more able to survive shipping than plants grown in water. In this case, the leaves will stay alive long enough for the plant to begin to put out its normal underwater leaves; then

Melting Crypts

Many species in the genus Cryptocoryne, known as "crypts," are excellent for low-light tanks, though they will grow faster with more light. Sometimes when crypts are moved to a new tank they "melt." The leaves die, and it looks like the plants just self destructed. In almost all cases the roots will send up new leaves, and in no time the plants will be back in full glory. So, don't root out melted crypts, since they will probably grow back very soon.

the original leaves will die and fall off. If the plant you purchase is a true aquatic, but its leaves remain rigid and upright when you lift it out of the water, it has been grown emersed and will have to undergo this transition to underwater life. If the leaves droop when held out of water, the plant was grown immersed and will not have this problem. It is also important to plant your plants properly. Some, like vals, need their crown above the surface of the gravel, and others, like anubias or Java ferns, should not be planted into the substrate at all, or their rhizomes will rot. If you buy bunched plants held together with a rubber band or a metal

Large snails can safely be removed from your tank if they are eating plants.

strip, you must remove that and plant the stems individually. Held together, the plants will rot from a lack of water circulating around them.

My Plants Are Full of Holes!

If there are holes in your plant leaves, or if they are ripped, shredded, or just plain missing, something is eating them. Many species of snails will eat soft plants, and a few types of apple snails will eat just about any plant. Fortunately, the most common aquarium snails, the pond snails of the genus *Physa*, usually confine their grazing to algae. I say "fortunately" because these snails are notoriously difficult to eliminate from the aquarium. Large plant-eating snails can simply be netted out and relocated if they are caught molesting your plants.

When it comes to herbivorous fishes, things are less straightforward. Many species will nibble and plant now and again without causing much damage. These include, among others, some barbs, loaches, catfish, and gouramis. Often they will munch on soft plants like anacharis and water sprite but leave tougher plants like vals, sags, or Java fern alone. Sometimes keeping the fish well fed with algae wafers or algae flakes keeps them from sampling the greenery. Still, it may be impossible to keep a specimen in a planted tank.

There are also entire species of fish that always fall into this category. Tinfoil barbs, silver dollars, and many cichlids will consume almost any aquarium plant. In addition, many cichlids and large loaches or spiny

Fish, or Plants?

Although you can certainly grow some plants in your aquarium, a lush underwater garden requires the focus to be on the plants. Once the needs of the plants are met, a few fish can be added.

eels love to dig, and they will uproot plants even if they aren't interested in eating them.

If it comes down to such a choice, you will have to decide to keep either your plants or your fish, or to set up another aquarium for either. The only other option is using plastic plants.

My Plants Are Turning Yellow!

Plants turn yellow in response to many different stress factors. Too little light and lack of nutrients are the most common reasons. If your light is sufficient, try using a plant supplement with potassium and iron in it. The importance of iron for plants is the reason why many planted tank enthusiasts use special laterite substrates. Laterite clay is high in iron, and plants growing in laterite will always have plenty of iron.

If recently acquired plants are turning yellow, they were probably grown under higher lighting than you are providing. Even if your light is sufficient for the species, if they are used to higher intensities, they may yellow when shifted to a lower light system.

My Red Plants Are Turning Green!

Plant leaves usually contain several different pigments, but they are typically overshadowed by green chlorophyll. This is why leaves turn color in the fall–when a leaf dies and stops producing chlorophyll, the other pigments become visible. Some leaves, however, appear red or purple when alive and healthy. They still have chlorophyll, but in relatively smaller amounts. If, however, there is insufficient light, most red plants will step up chlorophyll production and become green. This enables them to make better

It's easy to see the green spreading up the leaves of this swordplant.

use of the light that is available.

Thus, red aquarium plants generally require very high levels of light, and they benefit greatly from CO_2 supplementation also. Although beautiful, red plants are best avoided by beginning aquatic gardeners.

My Tank Doesn't Look like the Ones in Books!

A lush growth of aquatic plants is certainly a thing of beauty, but it usually requires special care and special equipment. You must realize that in a planted tank the plants are primary, and the fish are always secondary—and sometimes even absent. It is one thing to have a few nice plants in your tank, and quite another to produce a vibrant aquatic garden. The three major factors for success with aquatic plants are water, lighting, and nutrients.

Lighting and nutrients are interdependent; that is, if one is deficient, the other cannot make up for it. All the fertilizer in the world won't increase plant growth if there is not enough light, and the most expensive lighting system won't produce optimum growth unless you supplement your tank with CO_2.

Light, CO_2, and trace nutrients comprise a three-way limiting factor relationship. When balanced, they provide maximum growth; when one is available only at suboptimal levels, it becomes the limiting factor, and

Start Big!

Many people think that a "planted tank" is an aquarium with a few bunches of plants in it. Aquatic gardeners, however, typically place hundreds of plants in an aquarium. Aside from presenting a beautiful garden from the start, the mass of plant material rapidly uses up nutrients in the water that would otherwise fuel an algal bloom.

increasing either of the other two will have no effect. With a little experimentation, you can find out which is the limiting factor in your system and concentrate your attentions on increasing that instead of wasting time and money on the others.

Water

Most aquarium water will support plant growth, but only a few very tough species can tolerate extremely hard and basic water. A different few species are best suited to very soft and acidic water. In between, however, is a large range in which most plants will do well. If your aquarium setup is one with an extreme pH, you will have to research what plants can be used in it.

Water temperature is also an important consideration. Some plant species are actually temperate and will not do as well in tropical tanks. Similarly, only a few types of plants will thrive in the very warm water of a discus tank. Fortunately, most popular plants will thrive at regular aquarium temperatures.

Lighting

Most regular aquarium lights are not adequate for aquatic plants; both the intensity and the spectrum are wrong. Double strip lights, very high output (VHO) fluorescents, power compacts, and metal halide lighting are all used for aquatic plant systems, depending on the amount of light desired. Full spectrum bulbs rated at about 5500K give the best results. Lights of any type should be on 10 to 12 hours per day. Running them on a timer is easier, and it keeps the photoperiod constant.

How Much Light Do My Plants Need?

Low-light species like Java moss, Java fern, anubias, and many crypts (genus Cryptocoryne) can get by on one to two watts per gallon (0.25 to 0.5 watts per liter). Medium-light species, which include most of the common aquarium plants, need 2 to 4 watts per gallon (0.5 to 1 watts per liter), and a few more demanding plants require even higher wattage.

Higher wattages are needed if the tank is deep (more than 16 inches or 40 centimeters), or if the bulbs are not full spectrum.

Nutrients

The major nutrient for plants is carbon dioxide, CO_2. As light increases and the rate of photosynthesis goes up, the demand for CO_2 can exceed what is normally present in an aquarium. Supplemental CO_2 will make a substantial difference in this case, while in a setup with less intense light, the plants will be unable to use even the normal amount of CO_2, let alone any extra.

Strong lighting is required for healthy plant growth

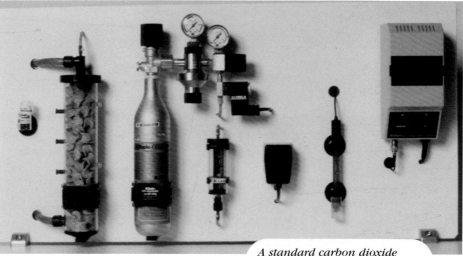

A standard carbon dioxide injection system.

Any aquarium with fish will probably have plenty of nitrogen compounds (ammonia, nitrite, nitrate) and phosphates for the plants. In fact, fast-growing plants can consume these substances, making them unavailable for algae, so having healthy plants is one of the best ways to prevent unwanted algal growth.

Trace elements like potassium and iron, however, can quickly be used up by a heavy planting. Besides the fact that this leaves your plants unable to utilize the light, carbon dioxide, and nitrogen compounds in the water, it gives algae a chance to pull ahead in the race for nutrients. Most serious plant growers change a third of the tank water per week, which replaces trace elements. When they use high intensity lighting and CO_2, however, they also often have to add supplemental fertilizers high in

potassium and iron, or use potassium fertilizers and an iron-rich substrate.

Help, I've Got a Jungle!

While not a terrible problem, aquatic plants can grow remarkably fast when conditions are right, creating a tangle of greenery. Pruning is a regular part of the maintenance of a planted aquarium. The cuttings can be used in another tank, or you can sell or trade them. Aquarium club auctions are a great way to spread the bounty around.

If stem plants have gotten leggy, you can trim off the lush tops and plant them to root, removing the rooted portions from the tank. Plants like Amazon swords or vals that reproduce with runners can be thinned by snipping the stems that attach the

not have a static look; instead it changes over time as different plants take turns in the spotlight.

In Conclusion

It is appropriate that we end this book about solving problems with advice on how to avoid potentially lethal ones. The aquarium hobby is fascinating and educational, and it is extremely safe as long as a few simple precautions are taken. Water is heavy, and it's dangerous when mixed with electricity. If you keep those two things in mind, you, your friends, and your family will be able to enjoy the beauty and wonder of tropical fish for many years.

In fact, almost all the problems you might face as a hobbyist can be avoided if you know about them. After all, helping hobbyists with problems is the focus of this book, but I would hope that even more people will be helped by reading about how to prevent any problems in the first place. With a little care, the aquarium hobby is a low-stress pastime, and the rewards for a little effort are grand indeed. Good luck with your aquarium!

103

plantlets to the mother plant and transplanting the youngsters.

Most aquatic plants can be severely cut back without harm, and the new growth is typically very lush. As with flowering terrestrial plants, pinching back new growth causes branching and fuller vegetation.

Some aquarists will plant a tank with an eye to how it will look in three or four months. A little sparse at first, it will grow in to create the masterpiece the planter had in mind. Other hobbyists plant a tank densely from the start, which helps keep algae at bay, and then they slowly replace some of the fast growing stem plants with other species. Either way, the aquarium does

Resources

Magazines

Tropical Fish Hobbyist
1 T.F.H. Plaza
3rd & Union Avenues
Neptune City, NJ 07753
Phone: (732) 988-8400
E-mail: info@tfh.com
www.tfhmagazine.com

Internet Resources

A World of Fish
www.aworldoffish.com

Aquarium Hobbyist
www.aquariumhobbyist.com

Cichlid Forum
www.cichlid-forum.com

Discus Page Holland
www.dph.nl

FINS: The Fish Information Service
http://fins.actwin.com

Fish Geeks
www.fishgeeks.com

Fish Index
www.fishindex.com

MyFishTank.Net
www.myfishtank.net

Planet Catfish
www.planetcatfish.com

Tropical Resources
www.tropicalresources.net

Water Wolves
http://forums.waterwolves.com

Associations & Societies

American Cichlid Association
Claudia Dickinson, Membership
Coordinator
P.O. Box 5078
Montauk, NY 11954
Phone: (631) 668-5125
E-mail: IvyRose@optonline.net
www.cichlid.org

American Killifish Association
Catherine Carney, Secretary
12723 Airport Road
Mt. Vernon, OH 43050
E-mail: schmidtcarney@ecr.net
www.aka.org

American Livebearer Association
Timothy Brady, Membership Chairman
5 Zerbe Street
Cressona, PA 17929-1513
Phone: (570) 385-0573
http://livebearers.org

Association of Aquarists
David Davis, Membership Secretary
2 Telephone Road
Portsmouth, Hants, England
PO4 0AY
Phone: 01705 798686

British Killifish Association
Adrian Burge, Publicity Officer
E-mail: adjan@wym.u-net.com
www.bka.org.uk

Canadian Association of Aquarium Clubs
Miecia Burden, Membership Coordinator
142 Stonehenge Pl.
Kitchener, Ontario, Canada N2N 2M7
Phone: (517) 745-1452
E-mail: mbburden@look.ca
www.caoac.on.ca

Canadian Killifish Association
Chris Sinclair, Membership
1251 Bray Court
Mississauga, Ontario, Canada L5J 354
Phone: (905) 471-8681
E-mail: cka@rogers.com
www.cka.org

Federation of American Aquarium Societies
Jane Benes, Secretary
923 Wadsworth Street
Syracuse, NY 13208-2419
Phone: (513) 894-7289
E-mail: jbenes01@yahoo.com
www.gcca.net/faas

Goldfish Society of America
P.O. Box 551373
Fort Lauderdale, FL 33355
E-mail: info@goldfishsociety.org
www.goldfishsociety.org

International Betta Congress
Steve Van Camp, Secretary
923 Wadsworth St.
Syracuse, NY 13208
Phone: (315) 454-4792
E-mail: bettacongress@yahoo.com
www.ibcbettas.com

International Fancy Guppy Association
Rick Grigsby, Secretary
3552 West Lily Garden Lane
South Jordan, Utah 84095
Phone: (801) 694-7425
E-mail: genx632@yahoo.com
www.ifga.org

National Aquarium in Baltimore
501 E. Pratt Street
Baltimore, Maryland, 21202.
410-576-3800
(daily 9:00 a.m. to 4:30 p.m.)
www.aqua.org

Index

(GFCI) devices and, 91-92, 92
heaters and, 90
pumps and, 84
securing equipment to prevent, 93
eyes, protruding or popped
 (exophthalmia), 56-57, 57

F

fat or swollen body, 56
fighting among fish, 64-65
fins, clamped, as sign of illness, 53-54
firemouth cichlid, 66
first-aid for fish, 55
fish illnesses, 45-57
    ammonia burn and, 48-49
    ammonia spikes and, 80
    bacterial infection, 54
    chlorine and, 80
    cottony growths and, 54-55
    fat or swollen body and, 56
    fluke infestation and, 49
    gill function impairments and, 48-49
    ich infection (white spots) and,
    49-53
    kidney disease and, 56
    life span and natural death vs., 81
    liver diseases and, 56
    lymphocystis infection and, 55
    nitrite poisoning and, 49
    odd behavior and, 53-54
    oxygen-low water and, 46-49
    parasites and, 49
    poisonous substances and, 80-81
    pop eyes and, 56-57, 57
    preventive measures for, 57
    quarantine aquarium for, 57
    salt as medical treatment in, 50-51
    sudden death of fish and, 79-81
    swimming problems (swim bladder
    dysfunction) and, 56
    viral infections and, 54-55

wounds and bites in, 55
fishless cycling, 16-17
flatworms, 37
floss for filters, 88
flow-through systems, 15
fluke infestation, 49
foam on water surface, 25-26

G

gill function and oxygen intake, 47,
 48-49
    ammonia burn and, 48-49
    fluke infestation and, 49
    nitrite poisoning and, 49
    parasites and, 49
goldfish, 56, 64
gouramis, 26, 38, 98
gradual stocking method, 15
green algae, 33, 34-35. *See also* algae
 blooms
green water, 22-23
ground fault (circuit) interrupters
 (GFCI) devices, 91-92, 92
guppies, 10

H

hairy algae, 35
hatchetfish, 74-75, 75
heaters, 89. *See also* temperature
    broken glass in, 90
    problems with, 90
    size recommendation chart for, 27
    thermostats for, 90
hiding behavior in fish, 61
hot temperatures, 27, 29
hydra, 37-38

I

ich infection, 50-53, 52
    dormant infection in, 52-53
    immunity of fish to, 53

About the Author

David E. Boruchowitz has been keeping and raising fishes for more than 50 years. The author of numerous books and articles, he also serves as Editor-in-Chief of Tropical Fish Hobbyist Magazine. David lives on a farm in New York State with his family and over a dozen aquariums.

Photo Credits

Photos courtesy of TFH archives

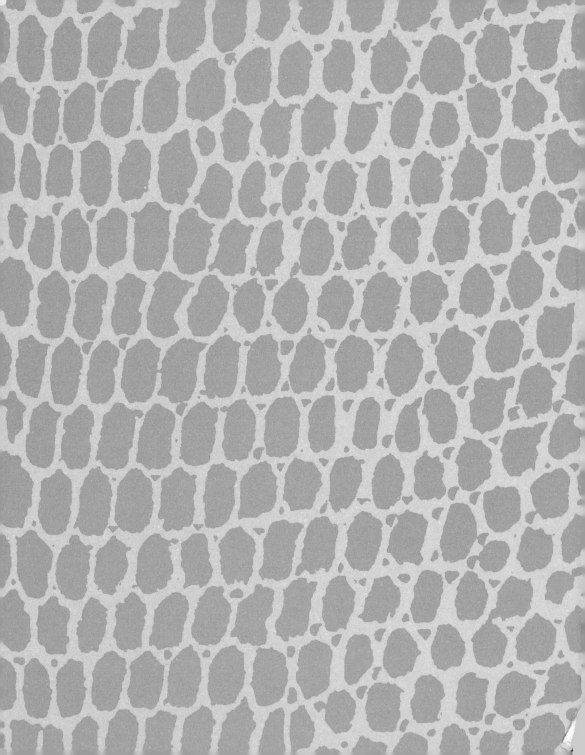